Wild
Singapore

Wild
Singapore

GEOFFREY DAVISON • RIA TAN • BENJAMIN LEE

In association with the National Parks Board, Singapore

Dedicated to the memory of Lady Yuen Peng McNeice (1917-2012).
An ardent supporter of nature conservation.

JOHN BEAUFOY PUBLISHING

Page 1: Boardwalks wending through the undisturbed mangroves give local residents access to one of Singapore's 24 Nature Areas.

Pages 2 and 3: A sign of increasing public enthusiasm for nature, volunteers take part in coastal surveys to monitor the marine seagrass communities that thrive in shallow waters.

These pages, main picture: Changi Point, once a favourite crossing point for tigers, now part of a public park.

Insets (opposite from top): Green Crested Lizard (Bronchocela cristatella); Straits Rhododendron (Melastoma malabathricum); Wild Boar (Sus scrofa); colourful gorgonian coral Sea-fans (Octocorallia).

Contents

Preface 7

Foreword 9

1 Singapore's Wild Past 10

2 What We Are Dealing With 34

3 Reefs, Rocks and the Open Sea 52

4 Mangroves and Mud 86

5 The Lowland and Coastal Hill Forest 110

6 Fresh Water and Freshwater Swamp Forest 134

7 City Living 154

8 Woodlands and Secondary Vegetation 174

9 Singapore's Wild Future 190

Acknowledgements 202

Bibliography 202

Index 204

MAP OF SINGAPORE

Legend

Forest, secondary woodland and dense vegetation
Open vegetation
Hill peaks
Developed land
Places of interest
Expressway and main road
Minor road

MALAYSIA

INDONESIA

STRAITS OF SINGAPORE

STRAITS OF JOHOR

SINGAPORE

JOHOR BAHRU

Tekong Island
Chek Jawa
Ubin Island
Serangoon Harbour
CHANGI
CHANGI INTERNATIONAL AIRPORT
Loyang
Pasir Ris
Tampines
Expo
Bedok
Katong
East Coast Park
EAST COAST PARKWAY
Paya Lebar
Geylang
Kampong Glam
Gardens by the Bay
Marina Bay
Rochor
Kallang
Little India
City
Dhoby Ghaut
Fort Canning
Clarke Quay
Chinatown
RAFFLES PLACE
SINGAPORE
Tanjong Pagar
Keppel Harbour
Harbour Front Cruise and Ferry Terminal
Sentosa Island
Palawan Beach
Underwater World Singapore
Mount Faber
Labrador Nature Reserve
QUEENSTOWN
Singapore River
ORCHARD ROAD
Novena
Botanic Gardens
Toa Payoh
SERANGOON
Ang Mo Kio
Hougang
Sengkang
Punggol
Bedok Reservoir
Serangoon
SELETAR
SELETAR AEROSPACE HUB
Sembawang
Yishun
Woodlands
No public access
Lower Seletar Reservoir
Nee Soon
Swamp Forest
Upper Seletar Reservoir
Central Catchment Nature Reserve
Lower Peirce Reservoir
Upper Peirce Reservoir
MacRitchie Reservoir
BUKIT KALANG
Singapore Zoo
Bukit Panjang
BUKIT TIMAH
Bukit Timah Nature Reserve
Clementi
West Coast Park
Jurong East
Choa Chu Kang
Kranji
Kranji Reservoir
Sungei Buloh Wetland Reserve
Lim Chu Kang
Causeway
Sarimbun Reservoir
Murai Reservoir
No public access
Poyan Reservoir
Tengah Reservoir
Second Link
Tuas
Boon Lay
Pioneer
Joo Koon
Jurong Lake
Jurong Bird Park
Jurong Island
Pasir Gudang
Bukom Island
Kuru Island
St. John's Island
Sisters Islands
Semakau Island
Sudong Island
Pawai Island
Senang Island
Raffles Lighthouse

N

5 km
5 miles
0
0

Preface

It was in 1960 that I first arrived at the Gombe National Park in Tanzania on the shores of Lake Tanganyika to study the chimpanzees living there. At that time their forest habitat stretched for miles along the lake shore and inland as far as the eye could see. Thirty years later the hills surrounding the national park were bare, the only trees remaining were in the very steep ravines. The soil had become infertile and eroded. There were more people living there than the land could support, and poverty was leading to the destruction of the last trees as people struggled to grow enough food for their families or make a living selling charcoal.

In the capital city, Dar es Salaam, around 130,000 were living – today there are more than three million. And most of the wild areas that existed then, with stretches of mangroves and tidal flats and areas of forest with abundant wildlife, have gone. Houses and industrial complexes have taken their place.

This story of deforestation, population growth and urbanizaton has been going on around the world. When Singapore was first colonized by the British in 1819 almost the whole island was covered with tropical forest, and the area was extraordinarily rich in biodiversity. But the forests were cut down for growing cash crops and by the 1880s only seven per cent of the original forest remained.

Today Singapore, a tiny island nation, is heavily populated and industrialized, and most Singaporeans enjoy a good standard of living. One might expect the wildlife and biodiversity to have suffered as a result of economic growth. Yet somehow it seems that economic development has been possible without devastating the remaining natural resources.

I have only visited Singapore on five occasions, but that was enough to learn something of government policies relating to the environment. I was pleased to hear that close to ten per cent of Singapore's land surface is dedicated to green spaces. That there are four well managed nature reserves rich in flora and fauna; well protected mangrove forests, tidal flats and coral reefs and a network of parks.

I gave up my full-time research at Gombe almost 30 years ago when I realized the extent to which forests were being destroyed across Africa and how rapidly chimpanzees and many other animals were being driven to extinction. I began travelling around the world to raise awareness about environmental and conservation issues – and I encountered so many people who had little hope for the future of our planet. If everyone loses hope, then apathy will set in and people, feeling hopeless and helpless, do nothing.

That is why this book is important for the informative text and beautiful photos show the full extent of all that has been preserved in Singapore. There is hope for the future. Human intellect and ingenuity are impressive, nature is amazingly resilient, and young people, when informed and empowered to take action, have incredible energy and determination.

But this book also points out that we cannot afford to be complacent. We must strive for a world that, as Gandhi famously said, can provide for human need but not for human greed. Each one of us has a part to play. Together we can work to ensure that the beauty of the wild places and wildlife will still be there for our children's children. And theirs.

Dr Jane Goodall

Primatologist and founder of the Jane Goodall Institute for Wildlife Research, Conservation and Education

The Jane Goodall Institute (Singapore) was established in 2007 to continue Dr Goodall's work with humans, animals and the environment. JGIS educates children and young adults about the importance of individual responsibility toward the ecosystem and supports them in taking action to improve their environment for the benefit of all.

GARDEN CITY FUND

Foreword

The reader may be forgiven for expressing initial scepticism at the title of this book *Wild Singapore*. In truth, there really is a wild side to Singapore, one that, although influenced by urbanization and human activity, also retains the natural beauty of Mother Nature and the benefits of her ecosystem services.

This book attempts and, I must say, quite impressively manages to capture the heart and soul of our natural heritage and brings it alive through engaging narrative and vivid photographs.

Every major tropical habitat from forest to sea, from mangrove to freshwater, from secondary woodland to park and garden is covered. But this is not just a beautiful book on the flora and fauna of Singapore, it serves a greater need to inform, educate and remind us of the imperative of conserving nature while the socio-economic needs of society are being addressed. Sustainable development is not a catch phrase. The future of mankind depends on the well-being of our natural ecosystems alongside socio-economic progress. The fact that more than 47 per cent of the island has a green cover, we have the only man-made offshore landfill at Semakau (with a regenerated mangrove, thriving reefs and seagrass beds, bountiful birds, fish, etc) that has been described by *New Scientist* as the 'Garbage of Eden' and two nature reserves (at Labrador and Sungei Buloh Wetlands) established as recently as 2001 plus a newly created second Botanical Gardens (Gardens By the Bay), all attest to the success of the sustainability framework mooted by the then Prime Minister Lee Kuan Yew, who half a century ago envisaged the concept of Singapore as a Garden City. The 50th Anniversary of the greening of the nations was celebrated in 2013. Several million shrubs and more than a million trees now grow on this 720 sq km island.

NParks and the three authors are to be heartily congratulated for producing a work that documents the natural and cultural heritage of Singapore. It is most refreshing to be provided insights on the beauty of nature in our midst and the numerous pressures exerted upon it, both natural and anthropogenic. While the City in a Garden may conjure up images of managed greenery, significant pockets of wild places and wild species of plants and animals still abound. I challenge anyone who says there is no wildlife in Singapore to visit the areas and places described in these pages, to prove to themselves the veracity of the title. Of course it won't be on the scale of Taman Negara in Malaysia or Tubbataha Reef in the Philippines but enough to please and surprise.

However, whether our existing wild life will be seen and enjoyed by future generations, depends on several factors notably the prevailing political, economic and socio-cultural climate of the time and aspirations of the people of Singapore to secure a healthy and dynamically sustainable 'live-work-play' environment.

Leo Tan PhD

President and Fellow
SINGAPORE NATIONAL ACADEMY OF SCIENCE

Chairman
GARDEN CITY FUND

The Garden City Fund is a registered charity and Institution of Public Character established by the National Parks Board in 2002. The Fund works with corporations, organisations and individuals to better engage members of the public through conservation efforts, research, outreach and education. For more information please visit www.gardencityfund.org.

Opposite: *Species of* Rhizophora *colonize shores with a fairly high sand content and have an extensive supporting network of stilt roots.*

1
Singapore's Wild Past

At the time of settlement Singapore was reported to be virtually untouched forest. From a township on the south coast, agriculture and dirt roads spread rapidly outwards, forest being removed for short-term cultivation of gambier, pineapple and other crops. As a result, much was lost before records began, but the work of famous naturalists made Singapore a key reference point on plant and animal life. Singapore's role in encouraging rubber and facilitating trade affected the face of South-East Asia forever.

Left: The first settlers in Singapore found a coastline indented with small mangrove creeks; various figs grow here, with the Mangrove Fern (Acrostichum aureum) *at left.*

Forging global links

On 26 April 1858 the Netherlands steamer *Banda*, captained by A.G. Bosch, left Jakarta carrying the mail that had been gathered from various islands in the Dutch East Indies. It arrived in Singapore on 30 April. There, the mail was transferred to the 1,200-ton, 400-hp steamship *Pekin*, owned by the Peninsular and Oriental Navigation Company (P&O) under Captain Burne (or Burns), which departed for Penang the next day, 1 May – the fastest transit time at any of the postal stops in Asia. From Penang the mail went on to Ceylon and, via a series of other vessels, to Suez, Alexandria – an overland journey by camel – Malta, Gibraltar and Southampton. From the ship's arrival there at 9 p.m. on the night of 16 June, it took less than nine hours to bring the consignment to the General Post Office in London just after dawn on 17 June. One letter, dated from Ternate, in the Dutch East Indies, was delivered to Charles Darwin at Down House in Kent on 18 June 1858. It was this letter, from Alfred Russel Wallace, that sparked the joint announcement by Darwin and Wallace of their discovery of the principle of evolution by natural selection.

Thus Singapore's postal efficiency, together with the astonishing network of Dutch and British transport companies, played a tiny but crucial role in bringing to the world the theoretical basis that underlies all biological, agricultural and medical sciences today.

Opposite above: Acacia auriculiformis *trees, here lining the old Lornie Road, were introduced early from eastern Indonesia.*

Opposite below: The site for the construction of the famous Bandstand in Singapore Botanic Gardens was prepared in the 1860s, surrounded by gravel paths and creeper-festooned trees.

Below: A deer fence had to be installed on the bank of Swan Lake in 1877. Lake and island still exist.

Wallace in Singapore

Singapore, then as now, was one of the key transport hubs in Asia. Wallace had first arrived in Singapore in July 1854, and departed at the end of October. The sequence of his travels is not made clear in his great book, *The Malay Archipelago: The land of the Orang-utan and the bird of paradise*, where he condenses all of his Singapore experiences into a single chapter.

'The island of Singapore consists of a multitude of small hills, three or four hundred feet high, the summits of which are still covered with virgin forest. The mission-home at Bukit-tima was surrounded by several of these wood-topped hills, which were much frequented by woodcutters and sawyers, and offered me an excellent collecting ground for insects. Here and there, too, were tiger pits, carefully covered over with sticks and leaves, and so well concealed, that in several cases I had a narrow escape from falling into them. They are shaped like an iron furnace, wider at the bottom than the top, and are perhaps fifteen or twenty feet deep, so that it would be almost impossible for a person unaided to get out of one. Formerly a sharp stake was stuck erect in the bottom; but after an unfortunate traveller had been killed by falling on one, its use was forbidden. There are always a few tigers roaming about Singapore, and they kill on an average a Chinaman every day, principally those who work in the gambier plantations, which are always made in newly-cleared jungle. We heard a tiger roar once or twice in the evening, and it was rather nervous work hunting for insects among the fallen trees and old sawpits when one of these savage animals might be lurking close by, awaiting an opportunity to spring upon us.

Several hours in the middle of every fine day were spent in these patches of forest, which were delightfully cool and shady by contrast with the bare open country we had to walk over to reach them. The vegetation was most luxuriant, comprising enormous forest trees, as well as a variety of ferns, caladiums, and other undergrowth, and abundance of climbing rattan palms. Insects were exceedingly abundant and very interesting, and every

day furnished scores of new and curious forms.

In about two months I obtained no less than 700 species of beetles, a large proportion of which were quite new, and among them were 130 distinct kinds of the elegant Longicorns (Cerambycidae), so much esteemed by collectors. Almost all of these were collected in one patch of jungle, not more than a square mile in extent, and in all my subsequent travels in the East I rarely if ever met with so productive a spot. This exceeding productiveness was due in part no doubt to some favourable conditions in the soil, climate, and vegetation, and to the season being very bright and sunny, with sufficient showers to keep everything fresh. But it was also in a great measure dependent, I feel sure, on the labours of the Chinese wood-cutters. They had been at work here for several years, and during all that time had furnished a continual supply of dry and dead and decaying leaves and bark, together with abundance of wood and sawdust, for the nourishment of insects and their larvae. This had led to the assemblage of a great variety of species in a limited space, and I was the first naturalist who had come to reap the harvest they had prepared. In the same place, and during my walks in other directions, I obtained a fair collection of butterflies and other orders of insects, so that on the whole I was quite satisfied with these – my first attempts to gain a knowledge of the Natural History of the Malay Archipelago.'

This first visit to Singapore in 1854 was crucial not only in giving Wallace an introduction to local nature; he also made the acquaintance of James Brooke, Rajah of Sarawak. Brooke was in Singapore at this time attending a British Parliamentary Commission of Enquiry into his activities and status. There were questions over how as a subject of Queen Victoria he had come to appoint himself as ruler of a foreign territory without his monarch's approval, his right and methods in doing so, and whether his suppression of piracy using British naval vessels was an abuse of official resources for personal gain. In spite of his troubles, or as a distraction from them, Brooke was most helpful and welcoming, and arranged for Wallace's 15-month stay in Sarawak.

Above: Swietenia macrophylla *were planted along Napier Road, now a 6-lane dual carriageway where they have been replaced by Rain Trees (*Albizia saman*).*

Opposite: *Wallace had an abiding interest in animal coloration and developed various aspects of theory on mimicry, camouflage and warning colours. The Green Crested Lizard (*Bronchocela cristatella*) is hard to spot amongst foliage, while the very slender body of the Red-necked Bronzeback (*Dendrelaphis kopsteini*) is inconspicuous within a twiggy bush. Here, crypsis beats camouflage.*

There, only three months into his visit (January 1855), less time than he had already spent in Singapore and Malacca, he wrote his first truly groundbreaking paper, 'On the law which has regulated the introduction of new species', the so-called Sarawak Law. In it he concluded that 'every species has come into existence coincident both in time and space with a pre-existing closely allied species'. It is remarkable that both this and the paper sent by Wallace to Darwin in 1858, two of his three outstanding pieces of theoretical work, were written while, or immediately after, recovering from bouts of malaria.

Wallace was back in Singapore in 1856, when most of his butterfly and beetle collecting was done. 'The mission home at Bukit-tima' and the wood-topped hills that proved such an excellent collecting ground have been identified as the area now occupied by Dairy Farm Nature Park adjacent to Bukit Timah Nature Reserve, as well as the forest now contained in the reserve itself. At the end of this second stay, in May 1856, Wallace managed to find at the Singapore

docks a local Chinese merchant's schooner, the *Rose of Japan*, with a Javanese crew and English skipper, that could take him to Bali and so towards his intended destination of Makassar. It departed on 25 May.

Above: The site of Alfred Russel Wallace's field work on beetles is now preserved around Dairy Farm, a building subsequently erected for a dairy cattle enterprise that continued into the 1960s. It is surrounded by secondary forest adjacent to 'the wood-topped hills' that proved such a fruitful collection site.

Opposite: The Dairy Farm building is now the Wallace Education Centre where school children and the public can learn about the history of nature conservation including Wallace's evolutionary theories.

The settlement of Singapore

Wallace is only one in a long series of naturalists who have made Singapore relevant to international science: Jack, Cantley, Ridley, Robinson, Kloss, Chasen, Burkill, Holttum, Corner we shall meet shortly. Thomas Stamford Raffles got his first view of Singapore towards the end of June 1811 and just before his 30th birthday, when he was on board the frigate *Modeste*, part of a fleet of 90 vessels on their way from Malacca to conquer Java. From 1811 onwards the Governor of Java, and later Lieutenant-Governor of Bencoolen in Sumatra, Raffles was working under the auspices of the East India Company, and was one of perhaps three key officials in South-East Asia, the others being Col. Bannerman (Governor of Penang) and William Farquhar (Resident of Malacca). Raffles must have passed Singapore repeatedly over the years, for by 1819 he had already long decided that it would form a better settlement than nearby Riau or Karimun.

When communication with superiors in India might take weeks, and with London months, individual enterprise was key. That January he outmanoeuvred his more cautious military colleague Bannerman in Penang, sent William Farquhar ahead in a merchant vessel, the *Indiana*, and joined Farquhar off Karimun on that vessel on 27 January. At 4 p.m. on 28 January 1819 they anchored off a fine sandy beach on the south side of Singapore, not far from where the modern city now stands. It was the first trumpet blast announcing the founding of modern Singapore.

Raffles was elected a Fellow of the Royal Society, knighted by the Prince Regent in 1817, was founder and first president of the Zoological Society of London in 1825, and died in 1826, a day before he turned 45. His biographer Maurice Collis has said of him that 'his elevation into a protagonist on the world stage was due to one great stroke. Just as in 1757 the few hours in Plassey grove turned Clive...into the founder of the Indian Empire, so Raffles's stroke at Singapore, the Lion City, in 1819, embalmed him forever as a man who moulded the course of history in East Asia.' Looking back, one might say that Singapore was the key to Hong Kong, and Hong Kong was the key to the opening of China. Yet as well as leading an extraordinarily busy life as an administrator and strategist, founder of the public service, town planner, legalist, developer of commerce and promoter of humanist causes, he had what virtually amounted to a parallel career in natural history, working with colleagues from the East India Company, such as Joseph Arnold and Thomas Horsfield.

Raffles published valid scientific names for the Long-tailed Macaque (*Macaca fascicularis*), Binturong (*Arctitis binturong*) (now extirpated from Singapore), Cream-coloured Giant Squirrel (*Ratufa affinis*) (another loss) and the Singapore subspecies of the Common Tree-shrew (*Tupaia glis ferruginea*) and Common Palm Civet (*Paradoxurus hermaphroditus musanga*). From his time in Java and Sumatra he published names for other well-known animals such as the Moonrat (*Echinosorex gymnurus*) and the Silvered Leaf-monkey (*Presbytis cristata*), and for several birds. Through his patronage of Arnold, Horsfield and others, his zoological and botanical influence extended through much of South-East Asia and thence back to Europe. His name will always be associated with the genus *Rafflesia*, the world's largest flowers that grow as parasites on forest vines. His paper of 1822 describing 168 bird species from Sumatra, Penang and Singapore is the closest approach to a first list of Singapore birds. No-one knows what Singapore treasures have been lost among the 100 packing-cases and the cages of living animals that went down when the *Fame*, carrying the great bulk of his collections towards England, caught fire and exploded off Sumatra in February 1824. Raffles' language teacher, memoirist and factotum Munshi Abdullah in his reminiscences written up as the *Hikayat Abdullah* might have exaggerated in stating that there were thousands of zoological specimens, stuffed or skeletons, but his report sounds reliable in listing three trunks of bird skins and several hundred bottles of snakes, scorpions and

Above: *The cupolas beneath a gigantic banyan fig at Fort Canning were designed by George Coleman, whose name is now commemorated nearby in the modern Coleman Street.*

Opposite: *Fort Canning's massive military establishment, built roughly on the site of Raffles' 1823 quarters, is now primarily used by the National Parks Board.*

insects preserved in spirit, all packed by himself during eight months of collecting in Singapore. Much more is thought to have been loaded at Bencoolen.

Astonishingly, more than 100 years earlier in 1703 the recently appointed Bendahara Sultan Abdul Jalil IV, created the Sultan of Johor because of the revenge killing of his predecessor, had offered Singapore as a personal gift to an English trader, Captain Alexander Hamilton. 'But I told him it could be of no use to a private Person, tho' a proper Place for a Company to settle a Colony on, lying in the Centre of Trade.' Hamilton obviously missed a trick but this demonstrates that Singapore was already on the trade routes and that the idea of setting up a colony there was not new to Raffles. By 1819 a key member of the Johor sultan's family and government, the Dato' Temenggong Sri Maharaja, Abdu'r Rahman, was resident in Singapore – he himself claimed to have arrived there only in 1811 with 150 followers, just a few months before the occasion in June when Raffles had passed by – making it one of three royal

centres in the Sultanate of Johor, and implying trade, settlement and the necessary agriculture to support it. From February of that year onwards the old Sultanate of Johor started to be divided. It had once extended as far as Pahang 400 km (250 miles) north and to the Riau and Lingga archipelagos far to the south.

Very little evidence remains of how Singapore's natural world might have appeared when it was founded in 1819. The island had contained a walled city belonging to the empire of Sri Vijaya, a great Hindu-Buddhist state that survived until the end of the 14th century. Under one or another transliteration of the Malay name Temasek, there are references to the island in 1292, 1330, 1349, 1365 and 1409. There are other references in 1430, 1511–12, 1577–87, 1612, 1703 and 1755. These include Italian, French, Dutch, Portuguese, English, Chinese, Javanese, Indian and Arab sources. Chinese traveller Wang Dayuan gave the first demonstrably eyewitness account in 1330 when a Siamese assault on Temasek was held at bay for a month. Wang used the name

Pan-tsu for what is now Fort Canning, a name thought to be derived from the Malay word *pancur*, signifying a spring. This water source on the west side of the hill was still in use in 1819. Excavations have revealed thousands of fragments of locally baked earthenware, Chinese impressed stoneware, porcelain greenware, whiteware and early blue and white Chinese porcelain (1300–68), as well as coins belonging to the Song Dynasty reigns of Yuanfeng tongbao (1078–86), Xuanhe tongbao (1119–26) and Jianyun tongbao (1127–31). Such coins are thought to have been brought in much later than their dates of issue, probably in the early 14th century. The Sanskrit name of the old city was Singhapura, the Lion City, an allusion to the holy city of Lord Vishnu. The idea that Singapore is poorly named, because lions have never occurred there, is facile. The lion referred to is the horned lion's head of Indian and Javanese art, an image that is sometimes combined with the earlier icon of a buffalo's head upon which there may stand a human figure. Such stylized images appear on tombs

and inscriptions in the region dating from megalithic times during the preceding thousand years.

If you look from the land, Singapore is a mere appendix to the Malay Peninsula. Certainly the willingness of the Johor Sultanate to give it up does not suggest that it was much valued. But if you look from the sea, as all the trading and warring parties over the centuries did, Singapore stands at a vast marine crossroads extending from Malacca and Penang to Jakarta, from Bencoolen to Indochina and the Chinese coast. Far from being a small insignificant village, it was a potential maritime strongpoint. The sea is the link that binds Singapore's history together. For thousands of years the sea provided a better highway than any on land, where forest and swampy ground hindered progress. All of the old Malay kingdoms and sultanates were aquatic powers. Across the sea, languages were shared and cultures and religions spread. Rivals were seldom landward neighbours, but seaward competitors for taxation and trade. It was across the sea that the spear was launched. In 1577 Mathias d'Albuquerque had put to flight an Achinese fleet waiting off Singapore, so as to escort a Chinese trading vessel to Malacca. In 1584 the Singapore Straits were chosen by the Sultanate of Johor as the place to block the passage of the Portuguese. It was from behind Singapore that Paolo de Lima swept out into the Singapore Straits to launch his attack on Bintan in 1587. The complexity of islands and shallow waters, free from most natural hazards and convenient to the old walled city, must have long been recognized as a safe harbour and a place to trade. Raffles' safe harbour was at the mouth of the Singapore River, called the Old Harbour. It was superseded by New Harbour, later renamed Keppel Harbour.

Many place names for coastal features important to navigators had been established very early. The rocks where Horsburgh Lighthouse now stands were already labelled Pedra Branca (actually 'Pedra Braca') in 1594 by the coincidentally named mapmaker Petrus Plancius. A decade later the map by the Portuguese mathematician Manoel Godinho

Above: Excavations at a portion of Fort Canning Hill have revealed thousands of pottery shards both locally made and imported, as well as ancient coins. Much more is likely to remain in areas yet to be investigated.

Opposite: The main gateway to the fort built in the 1860s on Government Hill, later Fort Canning, still remains, and some of the huge Rain Trees (Albizia saman) *may date from planting around the same time or shortly after.*

de Erédia in 1604 showed Tanah Merah, Tanjung Rusa, Tanjung Rhu, Pulau Ular and the Tebrau Straits using recognizable spellings, while either the modern Pulau Tekong or Pulau Ubin appears under the now unknown name Turuan. The name Sincapura appears on a 1596 map by the Dutchman Jan Huigh van Linschoten. Singapore was evidently well known to navigators of all nationalities for many centuries and the idea that it was a virtually uninhabited backwater might be partly because local building methods used perishable wood rather than durable stone. By 1819, only parts of an old city wall remained. The significant point is that settlement had been long and possibly continuous; not many voyagers would have gone inland to investigate and the native vegetation in 1819 is unlikely to have been as pristine as is often implied.

Early impressions

In June 1819, the Scottish botanist Dr William Jack, who was accompanying Raffles, wrote to his family that 'Seas of glass wind among innumerable islets, clothed in all the luxuriance of tropical vegetation, and basking in the full brilliancy of a tropical sky...I have just arrived in time to explore the woods, before they yield to the axe, and have made many interesting discoveries.' Two were of native pitcher plants, drawn and described, that Raffles urged be dispatched as curiosities to Europe. An estimate of the natural vegetation cover as it might have been before human intervention is of 82 per cent dryland forest, 5 per cent freshwater swamp forest, 13 per cent mangroves, and minor areas of other vegetation.

The impression given in school history books is that the island was inhabited by only a few hundred people, perhaps as few as the Temenggong's 150 followers, based near the existing town and close to Raffles' landing place. However, this is unlikely to be a complete picture. Chinese settlers may already have begun the cultivation of the gambier plant, and there were Malay smallholder communities. On the north side of the island were aboriginal (Proto-Malay) communities of Orang Seletar, based on the Seletar estuary but living entirely or almost entirely on board small fishing vessels. A cluster of their boats, moving about as a unit, would obtain fish, more particularly shellfish, crabs and lobsters, largely from the mangroves of the northern shore, the Johor coast and the intervening islands. Their catch could be sold or bartered in the old port and fort of Johor Lama, less than 1 km ($2/3$ mile) away. Similar fishing settlements, some of them Malay, occurred in creeks and river estuaries such as Sungei Berlayar on the south coast. On shore these settlements surely maintained areas of coconut for home use, this being one of the factors tying them to a particular mooring. One source suggests there may have been as many as 1,000 residents by 1819, consisting of 500 Orang Kallang, 200 Orang Seletar, 150 Orang Gelam

(all of these are well-known Singapore place names today), 100 Orang Laut, 20–30 Malay followers of the Temenggong and 20–30 Chinese.

The island was considered to be low and swampy. Contemporary accounts do not mention where these swamps were but, apart from the coastal mangroves, one can identify Mandai, Seletar and Senoko (remote from the more settled parts), Jurong and parts of the western coast now inundated by reservoirs as key areas that would have supported freshwater swamp forest. Apparently there was swamp forest at Changi near the east coast too.

Low hills were mentioned, and the remains of the ancient walled city were on the slopes and at the foot of what was dubbed Government Hill, later Fort Canning and now known as Fort Canning Park. Further inland, spreading cultivation and unpaved roads reached towards the foot of Bukit Timah, Singapore's highest point at 164 m (537 ft) above sea level. By 1827 two-thirds of the route from town to Bukit Timah was cultivated or reduced to grassland,

Above: Bukit Puaka, the tallest point on Pulau Ubin, gives a panoramic view of some of the historic uses of the island. Granite quarrying was a major activity on Ubin, while large portions of the island were devoted to rubber, coconut and other plantations. Now abandoned, Pulau Ubin provides a rustic getaway for urbanites in Singapore.

Opposite: Pulau Tekukor ('Dove Island') is one of the southern cluster of islands past which early navigators would have sailed to arrive at the inner harbour, now overlooked by towering office blocks.

although John Crawfurd, second Resident (in effect, governor) of Singapore on taking over from William Farquhar, had claimed that in 1819 'there was not an acre of its surface cultivated and not a dozen cleared of forest'. Gambier plantations were an immediate step after forest was cleared, and sometimes an excuse to take wood and charcoal. Pepper, nutmeg, cinnamon and cloves appealed to all, and contributed to the regional exports to Europe. Timber was the main construction material, trees being felled in the

Left: The Portia Tree (Thespesia populnea) *is a scarce tree along the coast, recognised by the five separate red marks in the throat of the flower. As the blossoms age they turn from yellow to dull maroon.*

Opposite: Putat Sungei (Barringtonia racemosa), *a mangrove associate, produces garlands of delicate, fragrant, night-blooming flowers that are pollinated by bats and moths. Now rare in the wild, it is listed as 'Critically Endangered' in Singapore.*

Below: One of the plants widely available in horticulture, but also growing wild in Singapore, is the waxy-flowered Hoya verticillata. Typically rooted in debris on the trunk or bough of a large tree, this climber is easily overlooked.

decreasing patches of forest and sawn on the spot, bodged roughly and then sawn using a saw-pit, which implies the use of long two-man handsaws. One man would stand on the log or on a frame above it, while the other stood in the pit below being covered by showers of unhealthy wood dust.

Part of Raffles' vision envisaged the natural world as a resource for commerce, with Singapore at its centre. Taking advantage of a plant-collecting visit by Nathaniel Wallich from Calcutta, he set up the first botanic garden on Government Hill in 1822–23, but without his driving personality to keep it going, it lasted only a few years. He and William Farquhar fell out at this time, yet they had shared an interest in both plants and animals, and their sponsorship of natural history artists ensured a surviving legacy in the works of Diard, Duvaucel, drawings in the India Office Library and in the Farquhar Collection now partly owned by the National Museum in Singapore. Raffles left Singapore for the last time in June 1823, having spent little more than 12 scattered months

there during his whole career. Farquhar, a struggling and seemingly difficult man, was relieved of his post and replaced as Resident by John Crawfurd. Farquhar eventually retired to Perth, in Scotland, from where he continued to wage a personal campaign for recognition of his role as founder of Singapore. The loss of both Raffles and Farquhar was fatal to these first steps in economic botany. As part of the new town's planning and development the house that had been built for Raffles was demolished in 1856, 1.2 ha (3 acres) of the hilltop were levelled, and Fort Canning was built there. It is possible that some of the biggest trees now standing in Fort Canning Park date from this time or shortly after. The garden was moved to its present site, which at that time incorporated a scrap of remaining primary forest, old cultivation, grassland and recently mined land.

By 1841 there were an estimated 50,000 coconut palms and 25,000 nutmeg trees on various estates and plantations, as well as betel, pomelo, mangosteen, jackfruit, durian, teak, pineapple, sweet potato, keladi and sugar cane. Other products included gutta percha, a precursor of rubber, initially tapped from trees growing naturally, and later from trees deliberately grown in plantation fashion. This was first brought to people's attention by its discovery in Singapore in 1842. Local artisans collected it by felling and debarking entire trees (a very wasteful method); the hardening sap was scraped off and softened in hot water so as to pick out the impurities. It could be shaped into any form, hardening on cooling, and re-softened and reshaped repeatedly if desired. Dr Montgomerie, the senior surgeon of Singapore, noticed it first being used for the handle of a parang (jungle knife), and commercially it began to be used for waterproofing cloth, shaping leather, making golf balls and even for ornamental mouldings around picture frames. However, most of its uses were soon overtaken by natural rubber and by synthetic plastics.

Outside the immediate boundaries of the town, details of which areas were developed remain very sketchy, but the main types of cultivation would not have differed much from what has been grown in the recent past: banana, tapioca and orchards of fruit trees including rambutan, durian and coconut, with some bamboo for light construction, and space around the single-storey houses for domestic livestock and the cultivation of herbs such as pandan and lemongrass. There is no evidence that rice was grown on a large scale (though padi fields were mapped in the vicinity of what is now Farrer Park to Balestier Road). Probably most of it was brought across commercially from Johor.

Commercial agricultural plantations were centred on the low hills in the immediate vicinity of the town, at Government Hill, Pearl's Hill and at what are now the grounds of the Istana (where nutmeg, cinnamon and clove plantations in the 1850s belonged to Charles Prinsep, whose name is now commemorated in nearby Prinsep Street). The central and southern parts of Singapore were so well settled that forest was confined to a few hill slopes and tops. At Serangoon Road, Mr Balestier's estate grew sugar cane.

Opposite: *The gates of the Istana (formerly Government House, now the official residence of the President of Singapore and working offices of the Prime Minister) open onto what was once Charles Prinsep's cinnamon plantation.*

By 1848 at least 27 per cent of the main island of Singapore was under cultivation. The crops grown were:

Crop	Hectares	Acres	Trees
Nutmeg	482	1,190	71,400
Clove	11	28	Not reported
Coconut	1,076	2,658	342,608
Betel	180	445	128,821
Fruit trees	420	1,037	Not reported
Gambier	9,802	24,220	
Pepper	1,058	2,614	
Vegetables	153	379	
Sireh	9	22	
Pasture	162	402	
Other	794	1,962	
(Sugar cane, rice, pineapple, etc.)			

Total agricultural land : 14,147 ha (34,957 acres)

Left: Cinnamon Cinnamomum iners, *once an important local crop, is still abundant as a secondary forest tree and can be recognised by its strongly three-veined leaves. Though the dried bark is the commercial spice, all parts of the plant are aromatic.*

Animal life

Less is known of 19th-century animal life in Singapore than of its plants. Many animal collections were not labelled precisely, and the position of Singapore as a trading hub raises doubt about the origin of many museum specimens nominally from Singapore. The extent and type of trade was remarkable, and the prices in Straits dollars seem cheap. In 1878 William Hornaday recorded that he was offered a fine Tiger (*Panthera tigris*) at $150, baby Orang-utans (*Pongo pygmaeus*) at $20 to $30, a pair of Proboscis Monkeys (*Nasalis larvatus*) at $100, a pair of full-grown Tapirs (*Tapirus indicus*) at the same price, Pangolins (*Manis javanica*) and Slow Lorises (*Nycticebus coucang*) at $2 each, and a Rhinoceros (presumably Sumatran, *Dicerorhinus sumatrensis*) at $250. Virtually all must have been imported from Sarawak (a three-day voyage) or from Malaya, though presumably local animals would also have entered the trade. It argues for the prosperity and available leisure time of the human population that there was evidently an interest in keeping exotic pets, though many of them would not have survived long.

Nor was the trade confined to mammals, nor to living specimens. Bird skins were bought by Europeans for museums, and feathers from Asian pheasants and birds of paradise from New Guinea passed through Singapore for the millinery trade of Europe and America. The pet trade continued throughout the next century. A photograph taken for National Geographic magazine in 1939, now in the archives of the National Museum of Singapore, shows the imported skins of five or six tigers, and of a leopard (*Panthera pardus*) (spotted, and therefore unlikely to be from the Malay Peninsula) displayed for sale in front of a roadside shop. Tortoises, a gazelle, golden and silver pheasants, mandarin ducks and a kangaroo make it evident that the trade was worldwide. But perhaps most astonishing was the tank owned by the Hon. H.A.K. Whampoa containing a growing Amazon waterlily (*Victoria regina*), a plant

that had only recently entered cultivation even in Europe. This alone shows the global reach of trade and the sophistication of local interests achieved within Singapore.

The reconstruction of knowledge about the past fauna of Singapore is littered with assumptions. A recent study describing catastrophic levels of extinction owing to the loss of natural forest assumes that bird life would have been just as rich in Singapore as it was in an equivalent area of lowland forest in the Malay Peninsula. Pasoh in Negeri Sembilan, for example, has more than 166 bird species of inland forest, 60 per cent confined to this habitat type. This is probably not a good model on which to base historical Singapore estimates. Penang, an offshore island with an area of 260 sq km (100 sq miles) and containing 50 sq km (19 sq miles) of inland forest, had a more reasonable 80 species. Phuket, admittedly in a different climatic zone, with an area of 520 sq km (200 sq miles) (close to that of the historical Singapore) and with 180 sq km (70 sq

miles) of inland forest, had 72 species. In percentage terms the losses in Singapore must indeed have been catastrophic, but in absolute numbers there may never have been as many bird species as is supposed, and their decline may have been less rapid if it had already started long before the 1819 founding of modern Singapore.

In 1841 the government engineer Major James Low made the throwaway remark that 'Happily the jackals imported from Bengal have become extinct', a sentiment with which we can heartily agree. His zoological knowledge was a little shaky – soils and agriculture were his forte – but he mentioned snipe, quail, plovers, magpie-robins, parakeets, wild boar, tiger, elk (presumably sambar deer), mouse-deer, a small deer the size of a bear (perhaps barking deer, but he seems to confuse them with mouse-deer), 'wild cats (beautifully striped)', civets and flying foxes.

Tiger stories abounded, even when tigers themselves did not. The first recorded tiger was noted on 8 September 1831 when a man was killed by one

on the road to New Harbour (later Keppel Harbour), near the Sepoy Lines at the base of Pearl's Hill. Shortly after there was a second death, and a sighting that November might have been of the same animal. In 1835 a tiger attacked a surveying party, landing on their theodolite. The theodolite was broken; the tripod-entangled tiger tripped; the men survived. Wild deer and pigs were so common in the forest that tigers were not likely to venture near human settlements, but the spread of gambier and pepper plantations reduced tiger habitat as well as bringing susceptible pedestrians within range of tigers. From time to time deaths reached or exceeded the estimate by Wallace that tigers on average took a man a day. Five men were killed in eight days in 1840. Three hundred died in 1857, according to Oxley, though only seven were reported to the police. Government was castigated for not doing more, and rewards for killing a tiger went up ($100) or down ($50) according to public pressure. In 1860, more than 200 deaths were reported to the police. A 'Tiger Club' was formed

by residents to shoot rogue animals. The death rate evidently rose or fell as individual tigers frequented a populated plantation, or as they roamed across from the Malay Peninsula (Changi Point was a well known crossing swum by tigers). It was high for short periods, and low or zero for months or years in between. Plantation owners had their own reasons to conceal deaths as these frightened the workers, disrupted the labour market and led to demands for higher pay. The last tiger known to have been shot in Singapore was at Chua Chu Kang in the 1930s.

Above: In September 1831 Singapore's first documented human kill by a tiger occurred near the Sepoy labour lines at the base of Pearl's Hill, now occupied by busy Outram Road.

Opposite: H.A.K. Whampoa's collection of Amazon waterlilies (Victoria regina) in 1877 were grown in a long tank amid terraced gardens shaded by fruit trees and other ornamentals.

Forests and plants

The Botanic Gardens have long been influential, and they have been administered first by two Superintendents – Lawrence Niven (1860–75) and Henry Murton (1875–80) – and then by a series of Directors from Nathaniel Cantley (1880–88) onwards. With the conversion of the post from Superintendent to Director, regional botany leapt forward. Cantley reviewed the status of forests, and Henry Ridley (1888–1912) put into force many of Cantley's recommendations. I.H. Burkill (1912–25) specialized in economic botany, Richard Holttum and E.J.H. Corner (assistant directors from 1925–49 and 1929–45 respectively) covered a huge array of interests from orchids, ferns and gingers to fungi and swamp forests, while Kwan Koriba (1942–45) reverted to cultivated plants. Murray Henderson (1949–54), John Purseglove (1954–57), Humphrey Burkill (1957–69), Chew Wee Lek (1970), Arthur Alphonso (1970–73), Ng Siew Yin (1976–88), Tan Wee Kiat (1989–96)

and Chin See Chung (1996–2010) have all had fundamental scientific interests and combined them with an increasing commitment to make the gardens a service to the Singaporean public.

By 1884, when Nathaniel Cantley produced his report on the forest resources of the Malay Peninsula and Singapore, the great majority of the natural vegetation had gone. Only 4,000 ha (10,000 acres) of natural forest were said to remain. Yet even into the middle of the 20th century areas such as the northeast, near Changi Point, were considered remote and difficult of access. Cantley's report led to the establishment of a system of forest reserves in 1884, the appointment of his successor Ridley, and a renewed seriousness on the part of government that led ultimately to the system of forest and agricultural departments in Singapore and the other Straits Settlements. Like the botanic gardens, the forest reserves have had a history of being shifted to suit the needs of other land users. They were briefly expunged altogether in 1936, but partly re-established

in 1939, including Bukit Timah where some of the last remnants of the primary forest not cleared by man remained.

Henry Ridley, born in 1856, arrived in Singapore as Director of the Gardens in 1888. Later he became Director of Gardens and Forests of the Straits Settlements, a much larger portfolio extending north to Penang and at a time when there was no Agriculture Department. Extensive collections made by him throughout Singapore and the Malay Peninsula still survive in the herbarium of Singapore Botanic Gardens, and it is evident that even if forest was officially reduced to only 4,000 ha (10,000 acres) just before his arrival in Singapore, remnants of a forest flora still lived on in many places. It was his role to implement many of the recommendations made by Cantley just four years before his appointment, including the delineation of the forest reserves. During his career Ridley published more than 500 papers and books, totalling more than 10,000 printed pages, as well as gathering

Above: *The reference books used by Henry Ridley, shown here at work at his desk around 1904, are still held in the Singapore Botanic Gardens' Library.*

Opposite: *A view of the Botanic Gardens jungle from the verandah of the Director's house in H.N. Ridley's time shows an* Albizia *on the left and* Bambusa vulgaris var. stricta *on the right.*

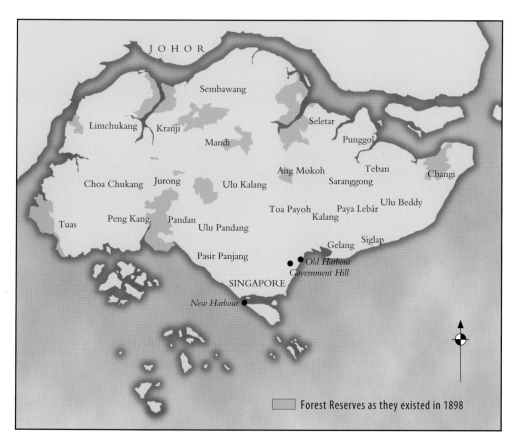

Left: *Map of old Singapore with various early place names (some curious spellings strike the modern eye), with Forest Reserves as they existed in 1898.*

Forest Reserves as they existed in 1898

some 40,000 herbarium specimens and making over 1,500 illustrations. Between the ages of 65 and 70 he published all five volumes of his *Flora of the Malay Peninsula*, more than 2,800 pages! And still more than 30 years lay ahead of him before he died in 1956.

Ridley is most famous for his role in promoting rubber (*Hevea brasiliensis*). He did not actually introduce it into South-East Asia, for specimens had arrived from Kew as early as 1876, but he was largely responsible for making it commercially viable by devising tapping methods, techniques for coagulation, using seeds as a source of oil, manuring methods and distribution of materials throughout the Malay Peninsula. Through the spread of rubber, he changed the economic and environmental face of South-East Asia forever.

Opposite: One of the second generation of rubber trees (Hevea brasiliensis) grown from original stock from the 1870s still grows in the Botanic Gardens.

He was also responsible for a great deal of the natural history notes to be compiled before the arrival of Herbert Robinson, who was based in the Federated Malay States Museum in Kuala Lumpur, and Boden Kloss at the Raffles Museum in Singapore. Ridley recorded a roost of 70,000 flying foxes (*Pteropus vampyrus*) using the Botanic Gardens jungle in one year prior to 1895, but such roosts tend to shift when disturbed and it is not clear how long this one lasted. Flying foxes were present until at least 1935, when Holttum recorded 'nightly visits of hordes of giant fruit-bats' to fruiting Tembusu trees *(Fagraea fragrans)*. Finally in the lead up to World War II, F.N. Chasen took over from Kloss and produced two foundational texts, his two 'Handlists' on the birds and the mammals of the entire region. All through this period the naturalists focused on the terrestrial flora and fauna. Shipping, piracy and trade were major concerns, but marine natural history was overlooked.

2
What We Are Dealing With

Surveys have shown that in spite of major forest loss in the nineteenth century, Singapore may retain between 25,000 and 40,000 species of plants and animals. This is primarily a sub-set of the flora and fauna of the Malay Peninsula, of which Singapore was part until the last few thousand years. The natural world is typical of that in the ever-humid, ever-warm tropics of South-East Asia, with high species totals in nearly all groups. The marine environment has apparently been much less affected by development than that on land.

Left: With good natural reefs accessible to the public, the Sisters Islands lie just off the natural shores of St John's Island. On the horizon are massive industrial areas on Pulau Bukom and Jurong Island and major shipping lanes.

The physical limits

Singapore's land area has changed greatly over two centuries. At the time of Raffles' landing, it is estimated that the main island covered about 524 sq km (202 sq miles). By the 1960s the total land area including offshore islands was 587 sq km (227 sq miles), but reclamation (mostly in the east, the southwest and along the south coast) has further enlarged it to 712 sq km (275 sq miles) by 2010. This 21 per cent increase may be a global record for real land creation by any nation, though of course many other countries have vastly exceeded this in territorial expansion by conquest. Singapore lies between latitudes 1° 10' (the southernmost islets) and 1° 28'N (the northernmost point at Sembawang), only 125 km (78 miles) from the equator and deep within the Intertropical Convergence Zone. At 104°E it is on the same longitude as the western tip of Lake Baikal, which is virtually at the mid-point of the Russian Federation (28°E to 170°W). Its antipodean point lies midway between the Galapagos Islands and mainland Ecuador.

Though Singapore's land area has increased so much within two centuries, some of it is not really land! Much of the early increase was due to the building of dams across estuaries to convert them to freshwater reservoirs; these were then counted as 'land' though still exceedingly wet.

The territorial seas around Singapore account for roughly another 700 to 750 sq km (270 to 290 sq miles). Historically there were 58 islands (many of them with fringing reefs) and about 20 more submerged or periodically submerged reefs. The number of islands has now been reduced to about 36, by reclamation and amalgamation, assigned to recreational, industrial or military use. The two physical links with Peninsular Malaysia are the 1,038-m (3,405-ft) causeway (constructed as a rail link in 1909, expanded to include a road link in 1919–23), and a bridge at Tuas known as the Jurong Second Link that opened to traffic in 1998.

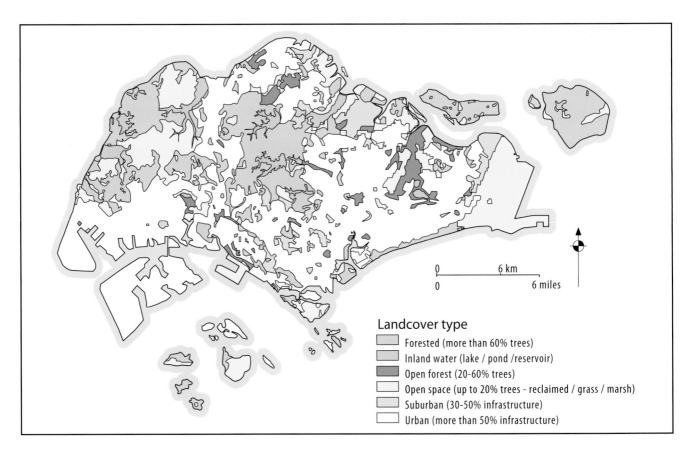

0   6 km
0   6 miles

Landcover type

☐ Forested (more than 60% trees)
☐ Inland water (lake / pond /reservoir)
☐ Open forest (20-60% trees)
☐ Open space (up to 20% trees - reclaimed / grass / marsh)
☐ Suburban (30-50% infrastructure)
☐ Urban (more than 50% infrastructure)

In terms of size Singapore makes an interesting comparison with some other well-known islands around the world.		
Hawaii (Big Island), USA	10,430 sq km (4,027 sq miles)	14.5 times the size
Stewart Island, New Zealand	1,746 sq km (674 sq miles)	2.5 times the size
Flinders Island, Australia	1,333 sq km (515 sq miles)	1.9 times the size
Singapore (2010)	712 sq km (275 sq miles)	
Singapore mainland (1819)	524 sq km (202 sq miles)	0.75 times the size
Montreal (Island)	499 sq km (193 sq miles)	0.7 times the size
Isle of Wight, United Kingdom	380 sq km (147 sq miles)	0.5 times the size
Martha's Vineyard, USA	226 sq km (87 sq miles)	0.3 times the size

Opposite: Sketch-map of land cover as of 2013; though merely an approximation this gives an idea of forest cover in the west, centre and offshore islands, and extensive areas of open secondary woodland.

Above: From the sea, under the vast sky, the main business district on the mainland is put in perspective. From the left are the still-wooded Pulau Tekukor, an abandoned ammunition dump, and the green hills of Sentosa which is a Disneyesque resort. Half of Singapore's national territory consists of sea; the 712 sq km (275 sq miles) of land nowhere rise higher than 164 m (538 ft) above sea level, giving no real scope for altitudinal effects on vegetation.

Warm and wet

Singapore has one of the least seasonal climates in the region and perhaps in the world. Mean monthly temperatures shift from about 24.7° C (76.5° F) during the coolest month (around December to January) to about 29.4° C (84.9° F) in the warmest months (May to June), less than 5° C (9° F) difference. The mean daily minimum is about 23.4° C (74.1° F) and mean daily maximum about 32.3° C (90.1° F). All such figures depend on the period over which they are averaged, so slightly different figures can be obtained from different sources. Night temperatures in the more rural parts can go down to 20° C (68° F), but more typical are pre-dawn lows of around 24 or 25° C (75.2 or 77° F) and daytime highs of 33 or 34° C (91.4 or 93.2° F). Morning mist is not rare in the rural parts, but is now virtually unknown in the city centre. Daily temperature fluctuations can be double the seasonal fluctuations. The city is hotter than the forested and agricultural areas, the difference being greatest (around 3 to 5° C [5 to 9° F], but occasionally as much as 7° C [13° F]) soon after sunset, when baking concrete retains its heat longer than the rapidly cooling vegetation.

Mean annual rainfall at Bukit Timah (a forested site) is 2,473 mm (97.4 in), versus about 2,190 to 2,300 mm (86.2 to 90.6 in) for Singapore as a whole (again the figures depend on the period over which information is averaged). There is significant variation – up to 500 mm (19.7 in) – in mean annual rainfall from place to place even a few kilometres apart. The wettest year ever recorded had 3,452 mm (135.9 in) and the driest year 1,484 mm (58.4 in) – only 64 per cent of the average. Mean monthly rainfall ranges from about 145 mm (5.7 in) in July to about 260 mm

Above: Singapore's main seasons are wet and wetter. Rain on the mainland may often fall in early morning from sea-clouds brought in over the Straits of Malacca, and in the afternoon often from clouds formed over the Malay Peninsula.

Opposite: Vegetation near the edges of some reservoirs includes remnants of freshwater swamp forest, valuable for conservation far beyond their tiny extent because of high species richness of plants and animals, many of which are confined to this habitat.

(10.2 in) in December, so there is a single, poorly defined wetter season during the northeast monsoon around November to January. But because precipitation on average greatly exceeds evapo-transpiration, the climate is classified as ever-wet, supporting year-round plant growth. It is a matter of wet and wetter, rather than wet versus dry seasons.

Remembering, however, that these are averages, there can still be extremes. The most marked of these may be caused by El Niño Southern Oscillation events (ENSOs) and their corollary, La Niña events, linked to prolonged rainless or rainy periods respectively, and intense bursts of rainfall that may be (but often are not) associated with La Niñas. Different weather events may concentrate rainfall in the early morning (e.g. the storm fronts known as Sumatras), in the late afternoon (convectional storms) or extend the overcast conditions through the whole day with periodic showers or steady light rain. A typical experience is of a few days wet, a few days dry, at any time of year, and short runs of similar events – for example, several days running with heavy showers at about the same time.

Temperature and rainfall events are critical to some plants. There can be heavy flowering by trees following a succession of cold nights, and ENSOs are implicated in triggering mass dipterocarp flowering. The Pigeon Orchid (*Dendrobium crumenatum*) is a classic case in which blossoms open nine days after a particularly cool night. In 1877 there was a 31-day drought, and in 1883 a 49-day drought; events of this magnitude affect all the vegetation, penetrating down to the understorey of the forest where there can be major wilting in the herb layer.

While not reaching the colossal daily maxima experienced in parts of monsoonal Asia, daily rainfall totals can be impressive. Over 500 mm (19.7 in) fell within 24 hours in 1978, and 152 mm (6 in) fell within three hours between 14.20 and 17.20 on 23 December 2011 (half of the month's total). On Sunday 29 May 1892 there were 232 mm (9.1 in) of rainfall in four hours, with floodwater 75 cm (30 in) deep at what are now the gates of the Istana.

Day length varies by less than 20 minutes between the longest and the shortest day. It has been suggested that this variance is inadequate to be used as a seasonal cue for breeding and other aspects of the annual cycle by birds and other animal life, though specialists point out that physiological

responses to day length are independent from conscious awareness of the change. Feeding time or available activity time can, however, be much more strongly seasonal than day length if activity of animals is constrained by heavy rain, meaning that their food intake is likely to be affected and hence their tissue reserves for breeding.

There are almost exactly 12 hours of daylight and 12 hours of night throughout the year, meaning that whether you are a day-feeding or a night-feeding animal, you do not have to adapt to big changes in the length of time you have to sleep and starve. Pity the poor creature of high latitudes that might face a 16-hour wait before its winter breakfast, but then gets woken at the crack of dawn in midsummer. As elsewhere in the world, the great majority (some 80 per cent) of mammals are nocturnal, but their behaviour is quite labile (liable to change); Sambar (*Cervus unicolor*), Lesser Mouse-deer (*Tragulus kanchil*) and Wild Boar (*Sus scrofa*) are amongst those that will often be active by day where threats and disturbance are low, but become more strictly nocturnal when hunted. Among birds that rely on vision, especially colour vision, and that cannot afford to crash in flight, fewer than 4 per cent of the Singapore species are nocturnal, but again there is an adaptable component among ducks, waders and some of the herons that enables them to feed at any time if water conditions are right.

Above: *Sometimes, the usually sediment-laden waters of Singapore can suddenly clear, so that living reefs, such as these on Sisters Island, are visible even at moderately low tide.*

Opposite: *The Pigeon Orchid* (Dendrobium crumenatum) *can flower at any time of year, gregariously, in response to low night temperatures; the blossoms last just days.*

Tides

Tidal ranges in Singapore tend to be quite small, around 2.1 to 2.5 m (6.9 to 8.2 ft) between High Water and Low Water Springs (only 1.5 m [4.9 ft] at Horsburgh Lighthouse), and 0.4 to 1.0 m (1.3 to 3.3 ft) depending on locality between High Water and Low Water Neaps.

There are two, slightly unequal, tides per day; and associated with these in a complex manner the waters of the Singapore Straits drift predominantly westwards and then predominantly eastwards at

Left: Mangrove muds are continually renewed by the deposition of sediment from both land and sea, and are therefore typically of recent origin. The trees behind provide excellent coastal protection.

speeds of less than 3.7 kph (2 knots) and usually less than 1.85 kph (1 knot). But where currents are constrained between islands, for example Sisters Islands and Pulau Tekukor, currents can be strong and hazardous.

Geology

The oldest zircon fragments in Singapore are dated to 2.71 billion years, more than half the age of the Earth, but these are mere fragments within a conglomerate of differently aged bits ranging down to 209 million years at the very end of the Triassic period. Most of Singapore's granites were not laid down until the middle Permian, between 250 and 260 million years ago, before the rise of the dinosaurs and just before the time at which the western slice of the Malay Peninsula began to grind into the eastern slice of Johor and Pahang. This movement was associated with the emergence of local vulcanism; there are no volcanoes close to Singapore today, but an ancient trace is visible as a small hill in Johor,

Opposite: Sandstone boulders erode out of adjacent cliffs, fall to the sea, and are rounded by wave action and partly embedded in a matrix of coral; while humans use granite masonry to protect the shoreline of Little Sisters island.

Bukit Penggerang, if you look northeastward from Changi Beach Park. Granites from this time occur at Bukit Gombak, Bukit Timah, Changi and Pulau Ubin (whose quarries supplied much of the granite for the Causeway).

Such granites occupy the central third of Singapore, north to Woodlands and Yishun. To the southwest, from Tuas to Sentosa, are conglomerates of sedimentary and metamorphic rocks making up the Jurong Formation. These are the ones that have the tremendous age range mentioned above. They are mostly below ground but where they are exposed, they tend to be crumbly, as in the coastal bluffs of Sarimbun, and of Labrador Nature Reserve. To the northeast, from Seletar to Tampines, is Old Alluvium sand and gravel, a 150-m (500-ft) thick layer deposited over the granite much more recently, around one to two million years ago, typically when sea levels were higher than now; and these have been the source of sands and gravels from Bedok and Tampines quarry.

The soils overlying these rocks are of more recent origin, caused by weathering and the growth of tropical vegetation over millions of years, supplemented by further deposits of recent Young Alluvium during short periods of slight sea level rise.

Singapore has never suffered significant earthquake damage, but slight tremors can occasionally be felt from geological activity arising

in the Indonesian 'Ring of Fire'. The earliest reports are of quakes on 24 November 1833 (attributed to Gunung Berapi in Sumatra); at some time in 1837 when a large wave broke onshore at Teluk Air; one on 6 January 1843 (also felt in Penang); and on 16 January 1861. The eruption of Krakatau was heard from 26 to 28 August 1883 (notably, residents were alarmed by the biggest global bang in recorded human history, at 10.00 a.m. on Monday 27 August), but undersea telegraph cables were disrupted and nobody in Singapore knew what it was until 29 or 30 August when a Dutch gunboat arrived with the news. Not long after, pieces of pumice stone, some as big as a hat, were found floating in the harbour, but there were no reports of tremors or damage in Singapore.

Above: Pulau Ubin's natural granite shoreline has been sculpted by nature into fantastical shapes resembling all manner of creatures. Use of laser and mass spectrometer technology on the boulders has revealed ages of around 95 million years.

History

Singapore has not always been an island. Sea levels fluctuated repeatedly through the Pliocene and Pleistocene, so that for long periods Singapore was part of the Malay Peninsula, and often simply an undefined spot within a much larger South-East Asian land mass joining Borneo, Java and Sumatra. More water locked up in ice at the poles and cooler sea water, meant lower sea levels and joining of islands such as Singapore to the mainland. The last such occasion was around 10,000 to 8,000 years ago, at the last glacial maximum. More recently as a result of warming, the release of water in ice and expanded warmer seawater, the sea rose to a level slightly above the present situation 5,000 years ago, and then settled back to what we see now. When the sea level was low, it would have been possible for people, and any animal life, to walk freely across what is now the Johor Straits. When the sea was just a little higher, Pulau Ubin would have been split in two, and

areas such as Changi and Mandai would have been submerged.

Because of the very recent isolation of Singapore from the Malay Peninsula, only a few plants and animals are unique to Singapore: they comprise three species of freshwater crabs, four plants (of which three have been lost to forest clearance) and an unknown number of invertebrates. The isolation has been brief, and for many mobile plants and animals isolation has been incomplete. The split of such a tiny island as Singapore from the mainland has meant that the population size of every species has been limited by available land area, so that many of those unable to make a sea crossing may have been experiencing gradual declines and there may have been a series of unrecorded extinctions prior to the arrival of humans.

More than 80 per cent of the coastline has now been altered by reclamation and coastal defences, with the construction of rock revetments, sea walls or other changes. On land, in readiness for building,

ground has been levelled and earth has been filled, so that new red impervious soil overlies the original, and some 20 per cent of Singapore now consists of mown turf. This is a far higher percentage than in any other country in the region. But the skin of new-filled earth is just a thin surface layer, below which the geological history of Singapore is still preserved: rich black soils beneath Jurong, alternating layers of sand and peat below Nee Soon, and deeply weathered sandstone beneath the busy campus of the national university – still lacking a geology department!

Above: Pulau Sekudu or Frog Island lies just off Chek Jawa, Pulau Ubin. It has a frog-shaped rock! According to legend, a Frog, a Pig and an Elephant held a race across the Johor Strait. They all drowned, the Frog turned into Pulau Sekudu, and the Pig and Elephant into Pulau Ubin. Pulau Ubin was originally two islands divided by Sungei Jelutong, becoming joined as the river was dammed for prawn farming. Pulau Sekudu is rich with marine life with sandy shores, large seagrass meadows and a reefy ring around a small lagoon.

People and their surroundings

The human population of Singapore in the mid-2010 census was 5,076,700 of whom 3,771,700 were residents (citizens and permanent residents) and 1,305,000 were non-residents (tourists, visitors, short term and contract workers, and so on). Population density was 7,126 people per square km, one of the highest in the world (after Monaco). Some 82 per cent of Singaporeans live in public housing (Housing Development Board apartments) and this has permitted very tight integration of public utilities, public transport and services making for economies of scale and high efficiency.

The largest agency responsible for conservation and greenery in Singapore is the National Parks Board, a statutory board under the Ministry of National Development, but municipal and town councils also manage some greenery, as do the Housing Development Board, Ministry of Defence and Singapore Land Authority. Marine affairs are largely handled by the Maritime and Ports Authority, Port of Singapore Authority, Singapore Land Authority (for the sea bed), and effective from April 2019, the Singapore Food Agency (for fisheries; prior to this, fishery functions were managed by the Agri-food &

Below: Park Connectors, in five loops covering much of the mainland, are designed to provide green corridors between existing parks and reserves, and to act as recreational features in their own right.

Veterinary Authority). By the beginning of 2018 the National Parks Board was responsible for management of 12,142 ha (30,003 acres) of land and fresh water surface. This included 3,347 ha (8,270 acres) in the four Nature Reserves, 2,807 ha (6,936 acres) in parks, open spaces, park connectors and playgrounds, 2,124 ha (5,248 acres) of roadside greenery including more than a million roadside trees, 3,749 ha (9,264 acres) of State land taken over from agencies and 66 ha (163 acres) of vacant State land.

The four Nature Reserves are the Central Catchment Nature Reserve (3,010 ha [7,438 acres]), Bukit Timah Nature Reserve (162.4 ha [401.3 acres]), Sungei Buloh Wetland Reserve (164.6 ha [406.7 acres]) and Labrador Nature Reserve (10.0 ha [24.7 acres]). In addition there are 62 Regional Parks and 310 Neighbourhood Parks (largely differentiated by size and proximity to population centres).

The Park Connector Network is a system of five loops and links between parks, through residential estates and connecting to rural areas, of which 313 km (194 miles) of walking and cycling trails had

Above: Structures such as the TreeTop Walk in the nature reserves provide safe access for children and the public to aspects of the environment that they would not normally see, improving awareness about nature in their surroundings.

been completed by 2010.

In spite of Singapore's small size, it is embarrassingly difficult to be precise about numbers of plants and animals, and it seems that the closer you look, the less certain the figures become. A rough estimate of the original vegetation is that it was 82 per cent dipterocarp forest, 5 per cent freshwater swamp forest, and 13 per cent mangroves (Corlett, 1991). By 1883 there were only 4,000 ha (9,884 acres) of forest (it is not clear whether this figure reflected only primary dipterocarp and freshwater swamp forest, or whether mangroves or secondary forest were included), and there are now about 192 ha (474 acres) of primary dipterocarp forest (all within the Nature Reserves) within a matrix of tall secondary forest. Some patches of swamp forest are also untouched.

The plants and plant-like forms

A total of 2,145 vascular plant species ever recorded within Singapore and its islands are known or presumed to be native (Chong et al., 2009). A further 209 are listed as weeds of uncertain origin. Another 1,826 have been listed as exotic (1,503 only in cultivation, 323 also naturalized or occurring casually in the wild), but if one considers all the species grown in Singapore Botanic Gardens and in the new Gardens By The Bay, the list of cultivated plants could be increased by several thousands.

Of the 2,145 native vascular plants (the ferns, fern allies, gymnosperms and angiosperms), some 1,506 have been listed as still extant (recorded now or at least within the past 30 years) and 639 have been listed as presumed to be globally (three) or nationally (636) extinct (Chong et al., 2009). Such numbers have to be taken as a rough guide, because every year species that had been presumed lost are rediscovered, new records of species previously not listed for Singapore are added and the 30-year cut-off period used to define 'extant' species is ever creeping onward.

The figures in the table opposite are not to be relied on, because there are many questions about the origins, native status and continued survival of many species, as well as the number that might have been present and been locally extinguished before scientific records began. They are only meant as a broad approximation to show the relative richness of different plant groups and the original literature and specimen records need to be accessed for greater reliability.

Below: Many plants and animals have been named after the site of their first discovery, including Kopsia singapurensis, *a small forest shrub that has been cultivated and is now widespread in horticulture.*

Plant	Total natives recorded	Extant natives	Introduced
Vascular plants	2145	1506	2035
Clubmosses and allies	12	8	3
Ferns and fern allies	156	125	29
Cycads	1	1	8
Conifers	2	2	25
Flowering plants	1974	1370	1970
Lichens	296	?	?
Mosses	168	8	?
Liverworts	94	74	?
Hornworts	2	2	0
Fungi	Unknown	?	?
Protozoa	Unknown	?	?
Bacteria	Unknown	?	?

Below: Pollination of the Simpoh Air (Dillenia suffruticosa) *by carpenter bees (*Xylocopus *sp.) will eventually yield fruits popular amongst many birds such as pigeons and bulbuls. This scrambling shrub is particularly common near lakes and ponds.*

The animals and animal-like forms

There is an estimate of some 40,000 species of native organisms in Singapore, by no means all named. If 2,145 of them are higher plants, the great unknowns are among the bacteria, the unicellular organisms, fungi and the invertebrate animals.

Just as for plants, the figures below for animal species numbers are not to be relied on. Wrong locality records, because of widespread trade in the 19th and first half of the 20th centuries, are probably even more severe for animals than for plants. Once again the original literature and specimen records need to be accessed for greater reliability.

Apart from the status of some manageably sized groups such as the vertebrates, butterflies, hard corals and sponges, where either a range of enthusiasts have tracked them for many years or they are the subject of specific recent studies, the numbers of species in many large groups, such as the mites and nematodes and many of the smaller insects, can hardly be estimated.

The top predators in modern Singapore, following the elimination of tigers, are Saltwater Crocodiles (*Crocodylus porosus*), Reticulated Pythons (*Python reticulatus*) and big raptors. The top raptors are of two main sorts: those feeding on fish such as the Grey-headed Fish-eagle (*Ichthyophaga ichthyaetus*), White-bellied Sea-eagle (*Haliaeetus leucogaster*), and migrant Osprey (*Pandion haliaetus*), and those feeding on small terrestrial vertebrates and invertebrates such as the Oriental Honey-buzzard (*Pernis ptilorynchus*) and Changeable Hawk-eagle (*Spizaetus cirrhatus*). The biggest mammalian carnivores now are Smooth-

Species	Total natives ever recorded	Extant natives	Introduced
Mammals	78	52	2
Birds	411	350	21
Reptiles	123	91	7
Amphibians	25	25	3
Freshwater fishes	41	34	34
Marine fishes	800+	?	0
All terrestrial invertebrates	20,000–25,000		
Butterflies	381	298	3
Moths	1,000 +	?	?
Dragonflies	126	?	0
Dipteran flies	Thousands	?	?
Beetles	Thousands	?	?
Spiders	c.400	?	?
Mites	Unknown	?	?
Nematodes	Unknown	?	?
Marine invertebrates	Unknown		
Sponges	125	?	0
Hard corals	256	c.155	0
Sea whips and sea fans	31+	?	0
Marine molluscs	550+	?	?
Crustaceans	450+	?	?
Echinoderms	68+	?	1

Opposite below: Wild Boar (Sus scrofa) are native to Singapore, were eliminated, but have recolonized by swimming over from Johor. The need for control of their numbers, and the way of doing so, is now problematic.

Left: Singapore's resident biological diversity is supplemented by migrants such as the Oriental Honey-buzzard (Pernis ptilorynchus) of which some spend their non-breeding season here while others move on to Sumatra.

coated Otters (*Lutrogale perspicillata*) (another piscivore, around 5 kg [11 lb]) and various civets (2 to 4 kg [4.4 to 8.8 lb], but civets are really omnivores that also eat a lot of fruit and invertebrates).

Local weights of crocodiles have not been recorded, but a big one could easily exceed 200 kg (440 lb). In Singapore even small ones are rare, and the bigger ones rely mostly on estuarine mullet as a staple diet, though presumably they would be on the lookout for any water- or land-based prey of suitable size. No recent attacks are known, but in 1887 the Raffles Museum 'received a crocodile, 11 feet in length, to which a melancholy interest is attached from its having recently devoured a native woman on the Ponggol River'.

Top body weights are scored by mammals that have all at one time or another been eliminated from mainland Singapore, but several have made a comeback. Adult Wild Boar (*Sus scrofa*) can weigh 80 to 120 kg (176 to 265 lb), Sambar Deer (*Cervus unicolor*) 160 to 260 kg (353 to 573 lb) and Asian Elephants (*Elephas maximus*) (that have swum over from Johor at least twice in history, in 1990 and 1991, and must have done so repeatedly in the ancient past) 2,000 to 3,000 kg (4,400 to 6,600 lb).

Though towns are highly unnatural habitats for tropical life, they may contain many natural pockets. Singapore has no natural lakes, and most open habitats such as grasslands would have been severely limited before the arrival of humans. As a result, many of the plants and animals seen around the houses and streets of the city are introductions from other parts of Asia and beyond. Native species are widespread, but reach their greatest concentrations in the forested nature reserves. Only in the sea has there been minimal change to species composition from human activities.

3
Reefs, Rocks and the Open Sea

The richness of marine life in Singapore's waters is comparable with nearby countries and for selected groups – such as hard corals – can greatly exceed diversity elsewhere. Populations of each species are small, and are vulnerable because they sometimes rely on recruitment locally, not recolonization by drifting in from neighbouring waters. Though underwater visibility is reduced by sediment, harbour activities seem to have had minimal impacts on the environment and dredging has never been required.

Left: Pulau Semakau, adjacent to Singapore's only landfill, has vast seagrass meadows with abundant Tape Seagrass (Enhalus acoroides). Volunteers of TeamSeagrass monitor this and other key seagrass meadows in Singapore.

Cyrene Reef: a marine gem nestled amongst the southern islands

The boat, 20 minutes out from West Coast Jetty on the mainland, has to edge forwards cautiously here, the captain adjusting the throttle back and forth, back and forth, because he cannot afford to let the slopping waves carry her forwards onto the sandy slope of the reef; not on a falling tide. Having felt his way as close as he dares, he will allow the little metal ladder to be put over the bow and hooked on to the rail. Now the reason for recommending tough rubber diving boots becomes clear; you have to step into water above the knee and find your footing on an unknown bottom. It will get worse underfoot later on.

A great orange-red structure, half-way between a gantry and a pillar, marks the eastern point of the reef. There's another, smaller, one over on the west point. The reef will only be exposed for three hours. It may sound like a long time but there's lots to explore on this 1 km by 500 m (1,100 by 550 yd) reef. Already the weed across the whole western side is exposed.

This middle section is beautiful fine yellow-white sand. The white bird that lands nearby is a Little Tern (*Sterna albifrons*). They have been breeding recently on Pulau Semakau, and on the mainland at Tuas. This sandy bank may look ideal for them, but of course it's only temporary as it's submerged at every tide. In the pools of water there are plenty of sand dollars and small starfish that may appear dead but are very much alive. You may come across a rather disgusting-looking sea cucumber, completely flaccid and inert and looking like a piece of discarded intestine. If it is put back in the water, it may recover some of its turgidity. The limpness is a sign of stress, and it will probably have drifted out of seagrass beds, which are a more typical habitat for it.

Amongst the seagrass

It is simply amazing to walk through one of Singapore's best seagrass meadows, but you should avoiding trampling on anything underfoot. You may see the extraordinary sight of

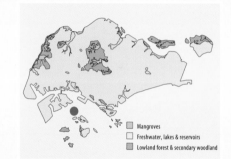

Mangroves
Freshwater, lakes & reservoirs
Lowland forest & secondary woodland

the wall-sided hull of a cargo ship passing less than a hundred metres away from you while you are standing on top of this submarine plateau, and yet all of the seagrass and all the algae seem totally unaffected. You may also spot an old rubber tyre half-buried, but it is already being incorporated into the reef by a thick growth of barnacles and soft corals that are spreading over it.

The last few centimetres of water among the seagrass will not drain away. These soft corals have found something firm to sit on and are steadily growing over the years, their rubbery bronze and – how shall we describe it? – purple? oily greenish? mustard-red? – communal body with a million iridescent green pinpricks showing where the individual polyps are to be found.

The rim of the reef has some really chunky hard corals. Once you have reached the edge, you can see how a cargo ship can come so close. The wall of the reef is nearly vertical, and although the visibility isn't good, you can tell it's no mistake to call this a plateau.

As you approach the rim, the egrets will move off, necks stretched out because they are not going far, just a few metres further along the edge. If they mean to make a

Opposite, clockwise from above left: *Cyrene Reef has among Singapore's best seagrass meadows and is fringed with living corals. There are abundant Knobbly Sea Stars* (Protoreaster nodosus), *individually identifiable by their spots, including many juveniles forming Singapore's most sustainable population of this species. White Sea Urchins* (Salmacis *sp., possibly* S. sphaeroides) *on Cyrene gather pebbles and shells held amongst their spines. A submerged reef, Cyrene lies within an 'industrial triangle' formed by massive petroleum facilities on Jurong Island and Pulau Bukom, the world-class Pasir Panjang Container Terminals and major shipping lanes in one of the world's busiest ports.*

longer journey, they will fold their necks in as they level their flight. Most of these are Great Egrets (*Casmerodius albus*), still with yellow bills and black legs, evidently not breeding. Where they do breed is quite a mystery, perhaps in the mangroves on the Sumatran coast, yet there always seem to be a few birds around whatever the time of year. Plenty of Grey Herons (*Ardea cinerea*) are found, of course, and the local speciality, a Great-billed Heron (*Ardea sumatrana*), perhaps the tallest bird in Singapore, which will be looking for fishes along the edge and gobies amongst the seagrass. Quite how these three big herons divide up the available food supply between them is still uncertain; but it could be a matter of indifference on Cyrene Reef when the critical factor is time to feed, not the amount of food.

Astounding marine life can be found on Cyrene Reef, a submerged reef surrounded on three sides by Pasir Panjang Container Terminal, Jurong Island and Pulau Bukom. Here are lush and vast marine meadows containing seven seagrass species. The only other shores in Singapore with as many species are Chek Jawa and Pulau Semakau. Cyrene also has the rare Noodle Seagrass (*Syringodium isoetifolium*), so called because it resembles stiff green 'mee hoon' noodles.

The only other place where Noodle Seagrass grows in abundance is at Pulau Semakau. Indeed, Cyrene probably has among the last few large seagrass meadows on the southern shores. Cyrene is especially rich in echinoderms: a group that includes sea stars, sea cucumbers, sea urchins, sand dollars and feather stars. Particularly abundant are the large cartoon-like Knobbly Sea Stars (*Protoreaster nodosus*). Cyrene is the only reef in Singapore where juvenile Knobblies are commonly seen. In fact, Cyrene may be home to the only sustainable population of Knobblies. Another spectacular sea star found at Cyrene Reef is the amazing Mamillate Sea Star (*Pentaceraster mammilatus*), a new record for Singapore. It was previously known only from the western Indian Ocean and the Red Sea, and might have been assisted here by shipping carrying ballast water. All too soon, you'll see the tide coming back in. It's time to return to the boat!

Below: *Cyrene lies just off Jurong Island, where nearly 100 petrochemical and chemical companies are located. And yet, Cyrene has clean natural sand bars teeming with sea stars and other creatures that are rarely seen elsewhere in Singapore.*

Fitting in the ships

It is about 15 km (9 miles) from Singapore to Batam, and only 5 km (3 miles) between the nearest of the Singapore islets (Raffles Lighthouse on Pulau Satumu) and its Indonesian counterpart. Hence the concept of open sea for Singapore looks more like the approaches to Sydney Harbour, New York or San Francisco than it does the ocean deep. The waters south of the mainland are broad and sheltered enough to take big shipping, and this has long been the world's busiest harbour, capable of mooring 800 large ships at any one time with a peak of perhaps 1,400 vessels depending on size. Only in 2005 was Singapore overtaken by Shanghai in terms of the bulk of cargo handled: 28 million container units as against 29 million by its Chinese mainland rival. This equates to an average 76,000 containers per day, so efficiency in handling the onloading and offloading is a key requirement for Singapore to maintain its competitiveness. The merchant fleet exceeds 3,100 vessels.

Squeezing this shipping into a relatively constrained area, and allowing for the other uses of the sea, such as industry, defence, aquaculture, recreation and diving, means that every part of the sea is covered by designated fairways and anchorages, or other assigned usages, and governed by complex radar, navigational guidance and markers. One might fear that such high intensity of use would have seriously degraded the marine life, yet there are some astonishingly pristine sites and sights.

Guidance of shipping is essential. Singapore's first lighthouse, Horsburgh Lighthouse, was completed on 27 September 1851, the tiny outcrop of rocks on which it was built measuring about 150 m (500 ft) by 60 m (200 ft). The rocks were known as Pedra Branca, 'white rocks' in Portuguese, presumably because of the droppings of seabirds. The reasons

Below: Enormous cruise ships regularly pass through the narrow channel next to the natural shores of Sentosa and Labrador.

Vertebrate animals in the open sea

With so much food imported, commercial fisheries hardly exist in Singapore except for cage-net culture of food fishes at spots outside the shipping lanes. Yet marine fishes are a key point of interest for coral reef divers – a popular and increasing hobby – and for anglers. Some of the main food fishes include families such as the *Carangidae* (jacks and trevallies), *Clupeidae* (herrings, sardines and shads), *Lutjanidae* (snappers) and *Scombridae* (mackerels and tunas). Though some of these are food staples for Singaporeans, they are largely imported fresh, frozen or tinned, but the same species occur in local waters. Seafood restaurants, though, may serve up a range of the more valuable wild-caught species such as groupers (*Epinephelus* spp.) and pomfrets (*Pampus* spp.), and cage-farmed giant Sea-perch (*Lates calcarifer*).

Fishes are the basis for a range of other vertebrate animals at sea, including perhaps the occasional sea-going crocodile. Birds will take only the smallest of fish. On the rocks around the base of Horsburgh Lighthouse is Singapore's only colony of Bridled Terns (*Sterna anaethetus*), around 80 to 100 strong. This is the most strictly maritime of the local terns. On a cluster of rocks off Changi is Singapore's only colony of another species, the Black-naped Tern (*Sterna sumatrana*). Each of these survives because the rocks are inaccessible. Little Terns, the only other locally breeding species, require not rocks but sandy bare ground, and nests can occur unexpectedly; one strange example was at the intersection of two busy tracks in a mountain biking trail.

Although nesting sites are limited, recent surveys have shown some gems among the pelagic birds. Aleutian Terns (*Sterna aleutica*), a species very poorly known anywhere until the 1980s, nest in Alaska and northeastern Siberia, and winter in Japan and the Philippines. They were first recorded in Hong Kong in 1992, and in Singapore waters from 1994 onwards. They are now known to winter regularly in small

for its construction were twofold: between 1824 and 1851 16 large vessels had been totally lost and another two grounded there; and it was a favourite place of attack for pirates, whose crimes included the theft of all goods, murder and the destruction of all traces of evidence. The granite base and walls were made from blocks cut from quarries at Pulau Ubin, and all the timber used was claimed to be from Singapore's forests. This first lighthouse stood 33.4 m (109 ft 6 in) above high water level.

In 1838 it was proposed to build a southern lighthouse at Alligator (now Pulau Pawai), Barn (now P. Senang) or what was then called Coney Island (now P. Satumu). The latter island, where the Raffles Lighthouse now stands, measured only 21 x 7m (70 x 22 ft) at the time, though it has since been enlarged. Rabbit (now P. Biola) and Coney islands were said to resemble those animals. Evidently the name Coney Island was transferred later to the northern island (Pulau Serangoon) now bearing that name. This second lighthouse was only completed on 24 May 1854 and was lit from 1 December 1855 onwards.

Above: Horsburgh Lighthouse, completed in 1851, safeguards shipping at the eastern entrance to the Singapore Straits.

Opposite: Raffles Lighthouse on Pulau Satumu, has been guiding ships through the busy Singapore Straits since 1855.

numbers, usually out of sight from the coast. Other species recently recorded include Wedge-tailed Shearwaters (*Puffinus pacificus*), Swinhoe's Storm-petrels (*Oceanodroma monorhis*) and three species of skuas or jaegers (*Stercorarius* spp.).

These bird species are typical of open water away from the immediate coastal zone, one of the reasons why they have seldom been recorded. Also under-recorded are dolphins and other marine mammals. Bottle-nosed Dolphins (*Tursiops aduncus*) (sleek and black) and Indo-Pacific Hump-backed Dolphins (*Sousa chinensis*) (brilliant pink when fully adult) can both be seen occasionally, herding small fish. Finless Porpoises (*Neophocaena phocaenoides*) are rarer, and there have been records of other small and large cetaceans – sometimes only as unfortunate carcasses – including Bryde's Whale (*Balaenoptera edeni*) and Pygmy Sperm Whale (*Kogia breviceps*).

Many early authors reported how calm the waters are around Singapore. William Jack was one of them, referring to the seas of glass. William Hornaday –

Above: *The Pomarine Skua* (Stercorarius pomarinus), *that forces terns to give up their catch, is very scarce in Singapore waters: this may be the third record.*

Opposite: *Small pods of Bottle-nosed Dolphins* (Tursiops aduncus) *can occasionally be seen in the Singapore Straits, especially when small fish are being harvested by artisan fishermen.*

Left: *A single site in Singapore waters houses a breeding colony of about 100 Bridled Terns* (Sterna anaethetus), *a pelagic feeding species.*

that American zoologist and collector who recorded the prices of live animals on sale in the 1870s – was another, who wrote of the sea being almost as smooth as a river. But striking incidents can occur. Sumatras are storm fronts that commonly originate to the southwest, generated by sinking cold air masses over the eastern Sumatran coast, and sweep onto Singapore in the early morning, bringing powerful gusts and intense rain. Seabirds flee before them. Water spouts are also known, several being seen in 2007 off East Coast Park in a single afternoon. Three in a row were seen on 7 November 1857. Typhoons generally run well to the north and east of Singapore, but the *Pekin* – that same P & O vessel that carried Wallace's letter from Singapore to Penang in 1858 – encountered one in October 1851.

When William Hornaday first visited Singapore in May 1878, he was disappointed that the local markets did not bear out the place's reputation for shells, starfishes and corals. But when he returned in December, he was brought shells and corals,

starfishes and huge Neptune's Cup sponges (*Cliona patera*) 'literally by the boat load'. He packed up several hundred specimens of corals, of 26 species, and more shells than he could spare time to catalogue. How many of these actually originated in Singapore could be questioned, given the regional trade in animals of other sorts. Vessels seem to have come in from Sarawak and possibly the Philippines with marine goods for sale. In 1842, for example, the *Belvidera*, registered in Bombay, was destroyed at Singapore while in transit with a huge cargo of pearls.

No-one in Singapore is more than an hour away from a magical sea shore. Though within easy reach, most of Singapore's shores remain an unvisited secret that few have seen. Most of the time, they are hidden by murky coastal waters at high tide. Singapore's underwater gardens are unveiled only during extreme low spring tides. Such windows of opportunity, however, are brief and happen during only a few months in the year, usually well before sunrise.

Fabulous at the fringes

At the edge of the land and sea, Singapore is rich in life. In places submerged at high tide, large schools of silvery fishes, squadrons of silent flat rays and other swimming creatures forage in a garden of colourful fluffy filter-feeding animals. At low tide, these creatures must either leave, or retreat into shelter when the shore becomes dry and exposed to air. But this is when sturdier marine creatures like crabs and mudskippers emerge to take their turn on the shore. This zone between the tides, the intertidal, can harbour such a wide variety of animals because there's lots of food and shelter here. The water is shallow, allowing sunlight to reach life-forms that undertake photosynthesis. These include seagrasses and, you may be surprised to learn, corals! These, in turn, are the basis for a bewildering explosion of life.

Gently sloping shallow shores result in a larger intertidal zone resulting in a more diverse patchwork of different habitats. On higher ground that is more often exposed by the tides, tough specialists find their niche. Further down, where it is seldom exposed except at the lowest tides, more delicate plants and animals thrive. Unfortunately, such areas are among the first to be buried by land reclamation projects. The resulting reclaimed shore is often steeply sloping with a narrow intertidal zone and thus fewer niches for marine life. Or it may be confined by artificial seawalls. But some marvellous natural intertidal areas have escaped development, while some man-made lagoons and seawalls are slowly being recolonized by marine life.

Why can't we see marvellous marine life every day? Although Singapore has two low and two high tides a day, the tidal height varies daily. Influenced by the gravity of the Sun and Moon pulling in alignment, an extra high (and extra low) tide occurs around the full and new Moon. Called a spring tide, because the water appears to spring up very quickly, a larger expanse of the intertidal is exposed at this time. It is during this brief one to two hours of low spring tide that we can glimpse deeper-water animals not

Opposite: The fierce Red-eyed Reef Crab *(Eriphia ferox)* has a set of cutlery perfect to deal with its snail prey. One of its pincers is an enlarged shell crusher, while the other slim pincer is used like chopsticks to tease out the snail flesh.

Below: Rich reefs and seagrass meadows are found on Pulau Semakau, even though it lies just across from Pulau Bukom, location of the largest Shell refinery globally in terms of crude distillation capacity.

adapted to being exposed for long periods. Good low spring tides in Singapore tend to happen before sunrise in April to September. At other times, the Sun's gravity pulls at right angles to that of the Moon. This results in a smaller difference between the low and high tide and is called a neap tide. A smaller expanse of the intertidal is exposed and we can then see only the more sturdy marine life adapted to frequent exposure to air. Nevertheless, enjoyable seashore exploration is possible on some neap tides during daylight, when guided shore walks are held at various seashore locations. No need to swim, no need to dive!

Unexpected spectrum north to south

Singapore's geography has given rise to a wider variety of marine life than might be expected on such a tiny island. The northern shores facing onto the Johor Straits are strongly influenced by the broad Johor River. Flowing more than 50 km (32 miles) down Peninsular Malaysia, fresh water from the river means that the waters bathing the northern shores are less saline and are loaded with nutrients. These are happy conditions for many specialist organisms, but they are variable. Heavy rainfall means more outflow from the river, and a specially wet period in February 2008 led to mass deaths of marine life on nearby shores because of reduced salinity. Recovery is still underway.

Corals and other marine life that require more saline and clearer waters are not as common in such estuarine conditions. These are more abundant on Singapore's Southern Islands and shores in the Singapore Strait. Thus the compact little island supports a wide variety of animals, some found mainly in the north and others more commonly in the south.

Tiny Singapore has representatives of all the major tropical marine ecosystems, many within easy reach. From mangroves and natural cliffs densely cloaked in coastal forests ringed by natural rocky shores, teeming sandy shores and seagrass meadows, to rich reef flats and wondrous submerged reefs. Even on the mainland, precious fragments of these natural ecosystems remain, while more untouched ecosystems can be found on its current 36 offshore islands and 20 or more submerged reefs.

Rocky shores

At first glance, especially in daylight, a rocky shore may appear barren. But if you look more closely, you'll find that a rich tapestry of life thrives there. Distinct zones on a rocky shore are fascinating to observe, as each plant and animal settles down on a spot to which it is best suited. Rocky shore dwellers have fascinating adaptations to cope with being baked by the sun at low tide and facing a tsunami of pounding waves at high tide. Countless barnacles pimple the higher levels of a rock, usually clamped up tight at low tide. Clustered on them are Drills (*Thais bitubercularis*). These are carnivorous snails that can pierce the shells of their victims. Drills lay brightly coloured cylindrical egg capsules among the rough surfaces of the rocks. A mosaic of Asiatic Tree-oysters (*Isognomon isgonomon*) may form a band beneath them.

A large wet rock often carries a film of tiny seaweed. This miniature meadow is home to tough little grazing snails and slugs, and the small predators, such as crabs, that prey on them. In wet, cool crevices and under stones, more creatures settle and hide. Rock pools provide a precious oasis where creatures may shelter at low tide. Nerite snails (*Nerita* spp. in the family *Neritidae*) often lay hundreds of little white egg capsules here.

Right: Like miniature Venetian glass balls, the delicately striped Lined Bead Anemone (Diadumene lineata) often dots hard surfaces on the northern shores. The anemone can reproduce by budding and is thus often found in dense clusters.

Where the rocks are less often exposed out of water, colourful gardens of hydroids, sponges and sea fans may grow. These can shelter seahorses, feather stars and other delicate creatures. At the low water mark, rocky shores may merge into other ecosystems such as seagrass meadows, sandy shores and reef flats and reefs.

The high rocky shore is usually much livelier during a low tide trip in the dark, before sunrise or after sunset. Crabs clamber around rapidly on pointy claws. The squeamish are often alarmed by swarms of Sea Slaters (*Ligia exotica*). Commonly mistaken for cockroaches, these are actually crustaceans. But even snails can escape rapidly. If you hear the rattle of falling marbles, these are semi-spherical Nerite snails suddenly retracting into their shells and dropping off the rocks when they are alarmed. Snails, limpets and slugs cling on to the slippery rock by creeping slowly on a broad foot. These are often well camouflaged; look for and follow the trail of 'processed food' that emerges from these feeding animals.

Singapore still has some picturesque natural rocky shores that formed beneath gradually eroding cliffs, cloaked in native coastal forests that produce nutrients for life on the shore below. Among the last mainland rocky shores are those at Labrador and Changi. Offshore islands such as Pulau Ubin, Sentosa and Saint John's Island also have some spectacular rocky shores. The many kilometres of artificial seawall surrounding Singapore are also settled by animals adapted for rocky shores. Onch slugs (Family *Onchidiidae*) are abundant but hard to spot. Small but resilient snails, periwinkles (Family *Littorinidae*) are common above the high water line. Purple climber crabs (*Metopograpsus* spp.) can be plentiful but only at night.

Below: Although resembling a plant, a sea fan (Order Gorgonacea) is a colony of tiny coral polyps. A sea fan may be home to an amazing variety of animals including snails such as ovulids, tiny shrimps, brittle stars and hermit crabs. Some of these small animals prey on the sea fan and resemble their host perfectly.

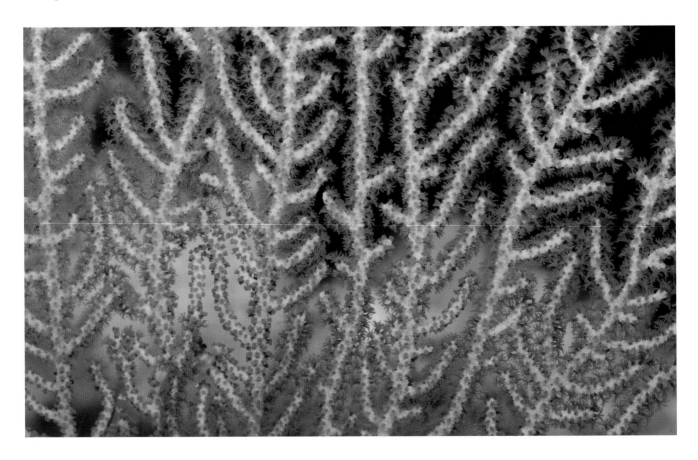

Above: Land hermit crabs (Coenobita *spp.) are abundant on remote wild shores, but rare on recreational beaches which are regularly cleaned of 'rubbish', and also the food and empty shells that hermit crabs need. Roaming away from the sea, some may even use the empty shells of land snails.*

Right: The large colourful Sally Lightfoot crab (Grapsus albolineatus) *is usually well hidden, its flattened body and legs slipping easily into crevices. Even at night, they are nervous and disappear rapidly with a clatter of sharp claws into the nearest hidey hole.*

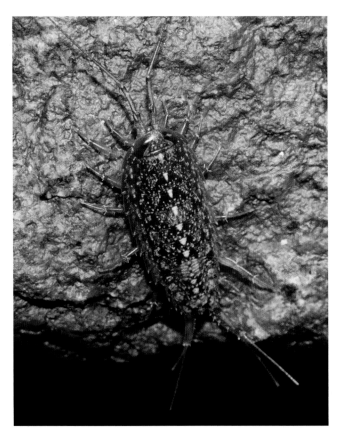

Left: Nervous sea slaters (Ligia *spp.*) often swarm the rocky shores. Although called sea cockroaches, they are not insects. They are crustaceans that are happy out of water, breathing. In fact, they will drown if kept under water!

Above: Commonly encountered under stones, the Ovum cowrie (Cypraea ovum) mother protects her egg mass with her large foot. So please don't pry off cowries.

Left: Colourful flowery soft corals (Family Nephtheidae) may fringe the base of rocks. Small false cowries (Family Ovulidae) often live and feed on them. These snails cover their rather plain shells with a fleshy mantle that is often textured and coloured to perfectly match the polyps of their soft coral host.

Opposite: Sponges are animals that often encrust the base of rocks on northern shores. They are found in psychedelic colours and fantasy shapes from encrustations, small balls and hollow fingers to bushes. Over 125 species are known so far.

Above: Polished nerites (Nerita polita) *come in a wide range of colours and patterns which allows them to blend among equally colourful rocks.*

Left: Tiny flat porcelain crabs (Family Porcellanidae) scramble madly *when a stone is overturned. As their common name suggests, they do tend to shed their limbs when stressed.*

Seagrass meadows

A miniature forest lies just beneath the waves of the intertidal zone. Unlike the more seasonal seaweeds, seagrasses are perennial and a lush meadow is an oasis in otherwise dangerous open waters. Sheltered from the worst of the currents and waves, hidden among the thicket of leaves, tiny creatures cling. Fishes, flat or skinny, slide easily among the blades. Crabs, shrimps and worms create safe burrows in the sediments stabilized by the mat of underground stems and delicate roots. Like Godzilla, towering shorebirds tread among the seagrasses snatching succulent morsels. Larger fishes patrol during high tide.

Seagrasses are true flowering plants that are adapted to grow submerged in shallow seas. They are not related to, and don't all look like, land grasses. Some are emerald green paddles the size of your fingernails; others are jade green ribbons that can be taller than a man. Some resemble delicate ferns, or lime green tubes.

Mothers of many different animal species love seagrasses. They lay their eggs on the leaves, on the stable sand or release their young into the thickets. Here, newborns and juveniles find food and safety. When they grow up, the adults may move on to nearby ecosystems such as reefs, or out to the open sea. Seagrasses are important nurseries for some of our favourite seafood. From squid to crabs, shrimps to fish, many marine creatures spend part of their life cycle in the seagrass meadows.

These meadows are vital to the gentle Dugong (*Dugong dugon*), which feeds only on seagrasses, and specifically on their rhizomes, not the leaf blades. Also called the sea cow, it is rarely seen in Singapore. But signs of typical Dugong feeding trails are still sighted occasionally on seagrass meadows

Right: The seagrass meadows on mainland Changi abound with astonishing marine life including many kinds of sea stars, candy-coloured sea cucumbers and colourful peacock anemones.

on mainland shores like Changi and offshore ones at Chek Jawa at Pulau Ubin, and Pulau Semakau in the south. Occasionally, Dugongs have been found onshore after being killed by a boat propeller. So far as is known, the population is tiny, possibly based in the Johor River estuary outside Singapore waters but roaming over a wide area to find sufficient seagrass.

While few animals can easily digest living seagrasses, decaying and dead seagrasses decompose into fine particles. This 'soup' of detritus feeds countless animals from anemones to filter feeders, and sand-shifting crabs and worms. The tides also flush these nutrients to adjacent ecosystems such as reef flats and reefs, as well as mangroves.

A seagrass blade is often carpeted with tiny algae and other encrusting animals. Larger seaweeds seasonally thrive in the meadows, entwined among the seagrass blades. Hordes of grazers small and large feast on these, and in turn are eaten by predators. Little grazers include snails, crabs and juvenile fishes that can peacefully feed at low tide, taking cover when large fishes prowl the meadows at high tide. Singapore has 12 out of the 60 or so species of seagrasses found worldwide and this is more than half of the 23 species that are confined to the Indo-Pacific. While seagrasses can be found on almost all its shores, Singapore's best seagrass meadows are found at Chek Jawa on Pulau Ubin, Pulau Semakau, as well as the submerged reefs of Cyrene Reef and Terumbu Semakau. These meadows are large (spanning 1–5 km [0.6–3 miles]) and lush with many different species growing together. The National Parks Board and Team Seagrass have surveyed 26 sites around the coast, of which 20 sites have three or fewer species of seagrass, but Cyrene Reef and Chek Jawa each have seven species growing together.

Above: The Feathery Filefish (Chaetodermis penicilligerus) blends perfectly into its meadow background. Although they can make a quick dash, filefishes generally cannot swim fast for long. Most rely on camouflage to avoid danger, changing colours and patterns to match their surroundings. Filefishes have tiny scales with prickles on them, so the skin feels leathery and rough, like sandpaper. They are thus also called leatherjackets.

Right: This Noble Volute (Cymbiola nobilis) mother is laying large translucent eggs. This predator "sniffs" out suitable buried prey such as a clam, which it wraps up in its huge foot. The volute then burrows into the sand and waits until the exhausted clam opens up to breathe, which can take several days!

Sandy shores

At low tide, a sandy shore seems like an uninhabited desert. But many animals live here and nowhere else: they are just very well hidden. In the waves, sand particles become abrasive like sandpaper, and the ground constantly shifts. Twice a day, water drains away with the tide and a sandy shore becomes a baking desert. Thus, most sand-dwellers, such as snails and clams, burrow deep into the sand to stay moist and cool at low tide, as well as safe from predators. Also hidden beneath the sand is a wide variety of worms: from fat Peanut Worms (*Phylum Sipuncula*) to long bristleworms that live in armoured tubes. Tiny holes or faint marks on the sand are clues to often much larger animals below.

Sandy shores are often bare of seaweeds and seagrasses because the shifting sand grains provide unstable ground and there are few nutrients. But shores which are a little muddy or silty will bear more plants. Some seagrass species are 'pioneers' and can grow on the edges of shifting sand bars. Their roots eventually stabilize the sand and may allow other seagrass species to settle there.

Together, sand grains form an entire galaxy of invisible life in the sand. As the tide goes down, each grain is surrounded by a thin film of water. Swimming about in this film are microscopic life-forms. These microscopic organisms are eaten by tiny animals, which in turn are eaten by larger ones. Many food chains on a shore depend on such humble creatures.

There are few natural sandy shores left in Singapore as most of them have been reclaimed. In 1958 a truant schoolboy could have crept from the main building of Saint Patrick's School on the south-

*Below: A sand bank may hold deposits of countless sand dollars! Often dismissed as lifeless, these velvety disks may be found even on reclaimed shores. The Cake Sand Dollar (*Arachnoides placenta*) is common, while the Laganum Sand Dollar (*Laganum depressum*), with a petal-shaped pattern, is rather rare.*

Above: Among the fierce predators of the sandy shore are moon snails (Family Naticidae). The moon snail has a large foot to bulldoze through the sand in search of buried clams and snails. It gets its food by secreting an acid to soften the victim's shell and slowly drilling a neat, bevelled opening using its rasping tongue. Mother moon snails embed their eggs in a 'collar' of sand. Each plasticky coil is full of living eggs, and only disintegrates once the young snails have hatched.

Opposite: The Common Sea Star (Archaster typicus) *is still seen on a wide range of sandy shores, with healthy populations on the shores of Cyrene just opposite the busy Pasir Panjang Container Terminals. However, populations in the North have been lost to reclamation and those at Chek Jawa (left), Pulau Ubin were decimated in the 2007 flooding event.*

east coast, walked across the grass lawn to the gate in the hedge, slid down a sandy path between the Morinda bushes and the sharp-leafed sedges, and found himself immediately on the beach. Today the school is 750 m (nearly half a mile) from the sea, and separated from it by the East Coast Parkway and by East Coast Park itself. The sandy shore has been displaced, and daily cleaning and sand replenishment hardly make it a natural shore any more. Among the northern islands, there are natural sandy shores on Pulau Ubin, the most famous being the one at Chek Jawa. Natural sandy shores can also still be found on Sentosa, Pulau Semakau and Cyrene Reef. Most of the sandy shores on the mainland are reclaimed land. But after many years, life has established itself and they now support quite an interesting variety of marine life. In the north, these include Pasir Ris (which means 'narrow sandy beach' in Malay), Changi, and the long stretch of reclaimed land on the east coast. Many of the Southern Islands also have sandy reclaimed shores.

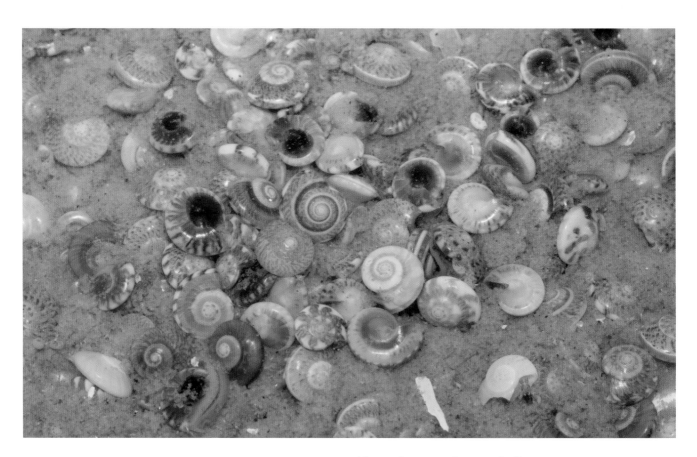

Sandy beaches on a tropical shore might well be thought of as ideal nesting sites for marine turtles, but in fact nesting records are quite scarce. Land reclamation, sea walls and seashore developments do not seem to be responsible for this; there has never been any substantial nesting by turtles, but every few years there will be a record of a Green Turtle (*Chelonia mydas*) or a Hawksbill Turtle (*Eretmochelys imbricata*) coming ashore to lay, or the discovery of an unexpected emergence of babies by some early morning visitor to the beach. But the scarcity of nesting is not to say that turtles do not occur; small or medium-sized individuals are seen quite often, especially in the shallow waters and reefs around the southern islands.

Above: Like buried gems, Button Snails (Umbonium vestiarium) *may be found in the thousands, lying just beneath the sand. The glossy shells come in bewildering colours and patterns. It is said that no two Button Snails are alike!*

Reefs and reef flats

Reefs are a magical wonderland where colourful trees and bushes are actually animals! Rocks that glow in the dark or look like abandoned brains are animals too. These are corals both hard and soft. Some can resemble delicately patterned plates, boomerangs and cabbages. Others, as big as a coffee table, are succulent leathery soft corals.

Sponges (animals too) come in clashing colours and fantastic shapes ranging from crumbly encrustations and fingers to roots, from small bowls to giant pots. In 1821 one of the most spectacular sponges, Neptune's Cup Sponge (*Cliona patera*) was described from Singapore. Pressures caused by shipping, sedimentation, land reclamation and pollution might have put paid to any chances of finding it again, but happily it was rediscovered after a very long gap by Lim Swee Cheng in 2011. This is just one of 125 sponges recorded from Singapore's waters so far, with perhaps more to come.

Right: Like other crabs, the Spotted Moon Cab (Ashtoret lunaris) mates face to face. Moon crabs have all their walking legs modified into paddles. Rather than to swim, these legs are used as twirling little 'spades' for digging so the crabs can disappear into the sand in an eyeblink.

Below: Rich reefs thrive on Pulau Hantu, next to massive refineries on Pulau Bukom. Large leathery corals (Family Alcyoniidae) may look like fried eggs, a pile of discarded rubber gloves, leathery giant carnations or floppy pinwheels. Each is a colony of tiny polyps embedded in a shared leathery tissue.

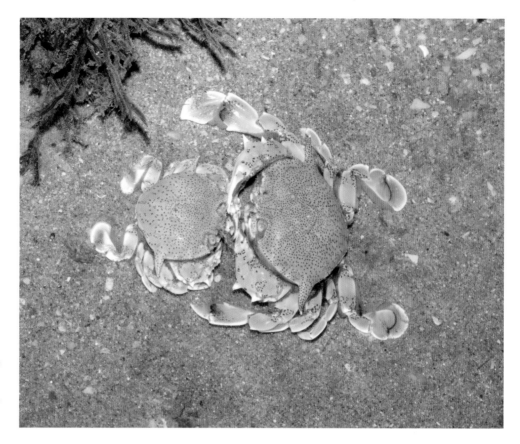

Tucked among the sponges and corals are psychedelic living carpets, feathery plumes like those that adorn Las Vegas dancers: these are sea anemones and feathered worms. At high tide, a rainbow of reef fishes swim among them. A closer look reveals delightful seaslugs (nudibranchs) that are cute as candy. These perfectly camouflaged animals are just as astonishing.

At least 20 families and more than 100 species of seaslugs have been recorded in Singapore, ranging from the very common Blue Dragon (*Pteraeolidia ianthina*) to the very rare Strawberry Seaslug (*Rostanga bifurcata*). We still lack a good field guide, or indeed any comprehensively assembled knowledge of these creatures, yet their brilliant colours and interesting behaviour make them the marine equivalent of butterflies, and their photographs can be collected and their habits studied. They are mainly carnivores, feeding variously on hydroids, sea anemones, sponges, sea pens, soft corals, ascidians, small crustaceans and other seaslugs.

Above: The chunky Ceratosoma sinuatum *has lobes that secrete repulsive substances.*

Below: Seasonally common, the iridescent Blue Dragon nudibranch (Pteraeolidia ianthina) *can capture symbiotic algae (zooxanthellae) which continue to photosynthesize and provide the animal with nutrients.*

Above: A slug in a pin-striped suit, Chromodoris lineolata *is among the many slugs that eat sponges, often specializing in particular sponge species. They can also incorporate the sponge's toxins into their bodies to repel predators.*

Left: A startlingly coloured nudibranch, Cuthona sibogae, *eats this hydroid. The bright orange feathers are a colony of tiny polyps.*

The Strawberry Seaslug may have been recorded only once from Singapore, but the species occurs all the way from the Arabian Gulf to Queensland. The other 12 species in the genus all have much more restricted ranges, outside Singapore's waters. Our only example feeds on sponges in shallow water, sometimes between the tidelines. It will produce a mass of microscopic red eggs in a complex spiral ribbon, laid on the surface of the sponge, and after nine days the small swimming veliger larvae hatch from the egg mass. They are thought to complete their development among the plankton before metamorphosing into adult form.

Unlike the stodgy, slow-moving Strawberry Seaslug, the Blue Dragon is a slim, elegant, wiggling piece of blue and purple iridescence, with long filaments that wave in the current. It specializes in feeding on hydroids, and this seems to be correlated with its shape, as other hydroid feeders are also slim and mobile, even when not closely related to each other. The outer surface layer of these animals

Above: The Blue-spotted Fantail Ray (Taeniura lymma) *is commonly seen. Other spectacular rays seen in Singapore include the Spotted Eagle Ray (Aetobatus narinari)*, a member of the Manta ray family.

Left: The Copperband Butterflyfish (Chelmon rostratus) *can be abundant in Singapore. Its large 'false eye' may fool predators into thinking that it is a big fish. And if a predator does attack, the butterflyfish unexpectedly appears to swim backwards. Its real eye is concealed by a colourful band.*

is immensely important. Some species contain single-celled algae that can photosynthesize, and their bright colours may generally be used in social interactions and to warn predators – they may contain toxins and may incorporate stinging cells from the hydroids or sea anemones they feed on.

Singapore's reef flats can be explored at low spring tide, and this is best done with an experienced guide who can ensure the safety of participants, and of the reef which can be fragile. You can dive the reefs too. The sheltered waters off Pulau Hantu harbour a rich variety of reef life that can be safely explored by divers. In fact, this is where many in Singapore gain their open-water certification. Although the water can be murky and visibility restricted to a few metres, the patient and sharp-eyed diver is often rewarded with sightings of special nudibranchs and small creatures. Sharks and sea turtles are also often spotted here. Other reefs are home to meadows of sea anemones and thickets of corals, while in deeper waters there are forests of sea fans and other soft bottom dwellers.

Hard Corals: trees of the reef

The richest marine areas are the coral reefs. Singapore is close to the Coral Triangle encompassing Borneo and the Philippines, and coral diversity is high.

Each coral is a colony of tiny animals called polyps, and each tiny coral polyp produces a corallite, an external skeleton made up of calcium carbonate that protects it and provides support. The polyp can retract into its corallite to hide from predators or to avoid drying out when the colony is exposed at low tide. The various colony shapes and surface patterns of hard corals arise from the way the corallites are arranged. What you see as a hard coral is the joined up skeletons of countless tiny polyps. They may produce a stony structure that is several metres in diameter, weighs tonnes and composed of hundreds of thousands of polyps.

A hard coral colony is therefore mostly made of dead calcium carbonate with a thin film of living

tissue that covers the entire surface. The tiny polyps are connected to one another through this common tissue. So it is a mistake to step on living corals even though the polyps are retracted, as you will damage the living tissue.

Like trees, hard corals also rely on sunlight for food. The polyps of reef-building hard corals harbour microscopic, single-celled symbiotic algae (called zooxanthellae). The polyp provides the zooxanthellae with shelter and minerals. The zooxanthellae carry out photosynthesis and share the food produced with the polyp. Although the polyps can also harvest food

Above: *Galaxy coral (Galaxea spp.) has long tubular corallites with a distinctive star-shaped tip. The spaces among these tubular corallites deep in the colony may shelter crabs, shrimps and other small animals.*

Above left: *An astonishing variety of hard corals can be seen on the richest reefs in Singapore on Pulau Satumu, the site of Raffles Lighthouse.*

Richness of Singapore's Coral Reefs			
Hard corals	Singapore	Indo-Pacific	Global
Genera	57 (84 per cent of Indo-Pacific total)	64 (67 per cent of global total)	95
Species	256 (52 per cent of Indo-Pacific total)	487 (67 per cent of global total)	731
Reef area	12 sq km	83,000 sq km	284,000 sq km
	(4.6 sq miles)	(32,000 sq miles)	(110,000 sq miles)
	(0.02 per cent of Indo-Pacific total)	(30 per cent of global total)	

from the water as they are animals, it is believed that the additional nutrients provided by the zooxanthellae are vital to hard coral health and growth. Thus clear waters that let sunlight through for photosynthesis are important for healthy reef growth.

The partnership between hard corals and zooxanthellae allows hard corals to thrive in clear nutrient-poor tropical waters. Like trees in the rainforest, hard corals provide the basis of life on the reef. Their hard structures provide shelter for small animals, a nursery for ocean-going creatures and they protect the shoreline from strong waves, storms and erosion.

Right: In the nooks and crannies of the Castle Coral (Pachyseris rugosa), *fishes may hide and fanworms, clams and other small animals may settle.*

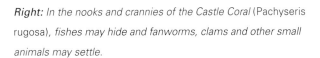

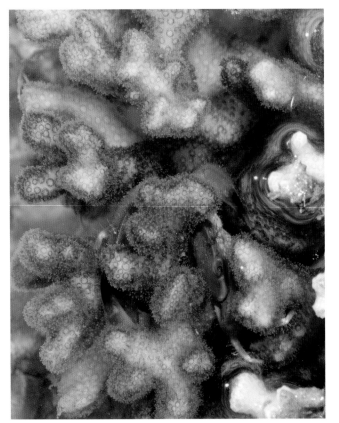

Above: Cave corals (Family Dendrophylliidae) are found in shady spots on the reef because, unlike most other hard corals, they lack symbiotic algae (zooxanthallae) and thus do not depend on sunlight.

Left: The tiny Red Coral Crab (Trapezia cymodoce) *lives only in Cauliflower corals* (Pocillopora spp.). *It feeds on the mucus produced by the coral and, in turn, nips at predators trying to feed on the coral.*

Coral bleaching

Much of the colour of coral polyps comes from the zooxanthellae that they harbour. When corals are stressed, there may be mass loss of zooxanthellae in a hard coral colony. As a result, the underlying white skeleton shows through the now transparent polyps. The coral colony thus appears white or 'bleached'. Without the food provided by the lost zooxanthellae, the polyps will be stressed and prone to diseases. Skeleton production and reproduction are also affected. Once the cause of bleaching is removed, however, some polyps may eventually regain zooxanthellae (which live freely in the water) and thus recover their colour and health. But prolonged bleaching can seriously damage large sections of a reef as it leads to the death of many polyps. Bleaching doesn't only happen to hard corals, but may also affect other animals that have a similar relationship with zooxanthellae, such as sea anemones, soft corals and giant clams.

Factors believed to cause bleaching include temperature fluctuations (too high or too low), excessive exposure to ultraviolet light, excessive sedimentation in the water, changes in salinity (such as due to flooding), pollution, oil spills and disease. It is generally believed that bleaching is related to unusual prolonged temperature increases in the sea water. Hard corals harbouring zooxanthellae live close to the upper limit of temperature tolerance. Thus a temperature increase of even 1–2°C can result in bleaching. Like many other reefs around the world, Singapore's reefs suffered mass bleaching in 1998 and 2010. It is believed that global warming will lead to more frequent occurrences of mass bleaching, but there may also have been some localized adaptation to temperature stress.

Above: The Broad-barred Acropora Goby (Gobiodon histrio) *lives only among the branches of Acropora corals (Acropora spp.) It stays even when the coral is exposed at low tide because it can breathe air!*

Orgy in the sea!

Once a year, a massive marine orgasm takes places silently in Singapore's waters. Romantically, this generally happens on the fourth month, four days after the full moon. Limited spawning can also occur during the third month. Called coral mass spawning, this is when a vast proportion of corals of many different species release their eggs and sperm all at the same time. The eggs and sperm drift to the water surface in bundles or packets which then burst open and fertilization occurs. While enormous quantities of eggs and sperm are released during a mass spawn, most do not survive. Hordes of marine creatures gorge on the spawn, from fishes and crabs to jellyfishes. As the tiny coral larvae develop, they have to survive the countless predators that constantly sieve the water for plankton and edible bits. Excessive sedimentation can also interfere with fertilization and other aspects of coral larvae survival and successful settlement.

It was in Singapore that coral mass spawning was first recorded in the tropics by researchers from the National University of Singapore in 2002. Previously, this behaviour had been thought to occur only outside the tropics where temperature triggers are more pronounced. In Singapore, coral mass spawning involves up to 18 different coral species from ten genera and five families. The fact that Singapore's corals mass spawn shows that its reefs are functioning well. According to biologist James Guest, the number of coral species that mass spawn is 'as high as on other Indo-Pacific reefs, like the Great Barrier Reef. This shows how rich Singapore's natural heritage is. We can find right at our doorstep: diverse, functional and fascinating coral reefs that people would normally associate only with countries like Australia.'

Above: Elegant Yellow-lipped Sea Kraits (Laticauda colubrina) *are highly venomous, although they are harmless unless provoked.*

Left: The False Clown Anemonefish (Amphiprion ocellaris) *is commonly seen in Singapore, usually in the Giant Carpet Anemone* (Stichodactyla gigantea). *The largest fish in the anemone is the breeding female and the next largest the dominant male. Should the female die, the male turns into a female and the next largest fish becomes her mate.*

Above: Colourful and fearless, swimming crabs (Family Portunidae) are common. Swift and agile swimmers, they snag fast-moving fish with spiny pincers. But they will also eat tough creatures like this heart urchin.

Left: Within the thickets of the underwater forest, life and death struggles happen silently. This tiny snake-like Carpet Eel-blenny (Congrogadus subducens) *lurking among the 'branches' of a leathery soft coral (Family Alcyoniidae) has snapped up a Tropical Silverside* (Atherinomorus duodecimalis).

4
Mangroves and Mud

Mangroves support an array of strange creatures from tree-climbing crabs to fish that spit. Reduced in size by both landward and seaward development pressures, Singapore's mangroves are still unusual in not being exploited commercially, so that rare pristine examples can be found supporting globally significant percentages of some endangered species. Mangrove Pittas (Pitta megarhyncha) and Great-billed Herons (Ardea sumatrana) can be found in close association with some of the most threatened mangrove trees. New species of crabs, flies and bees continue to be discovered.

Left: In constructing the Semakau Landfill, stretches of Pulau Semakau's natural mangroves with large mature trees such as these were spared.

Sungei Buloh: mud paradise for waders on the northwest coast

This morning the tide is still going out, down the estuary, a steady flow of thick brown water. Though this is called a river, it is broad and short; most of the water flow is tidal, since the catchment area behind is small, capturing little rainfall that flows into a few streams and drains feeding its headwaters.

The tide itself is strong, and archer fish (*Toxotes* spp.), some of them a hefty 20 cm (8 in) long, have positioned themselves just upstream of the pillars supporting the bridge. You can look over the hand-rail straight down onto their silvery-gold backs, and see the great black patches along their flanks. They put their heads to the current, tails to the pillar where the water divides around it. This is the place where they need to expend the least energy in order to stay put. Every pillar has one or two in position. In these conditions they cannot feed – later, in more placid spots where the mangrove foliage hangs close over the water, they will be on the look-out for insects or other bits of food that might accidentally have fallen onto the water surface. Sometimes they take a more proactive approach, spotting movement just overhead, and spit out a gobbet of water to knock the insect down.

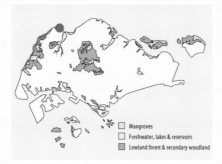

Other fish are here too; skinny translucent pipefish (family Syngnathidae) each with one iridescent spot of blue on its skull and one on the snout. Over there in shallower water is a swirl and a ripple from a small group of Greenback Mullet (*Liza subviridis*), and right at the edge the strange circular hollows being left behind by the falling water have been made as courting and mating spots by one of the introduced tilapia species, the Green Chromide (*Etroplus suratensis*). Each is owned by a protective male.

Lying in wait

Right back there under the branches, a single golden eye protrudes from the water; if you look a handspan to the right, you can see nostrils! It's a young Estuarine Crocodile (*Crocodylus porosus*). He's often at this spot, waiting to see if the mullet come close enough to be snapped up. That eye looks absolutely still, but you might notice that as the tide recedes and the water creeps down the muddy slope, the eye remains exactly the same distance from the edge. The crocodile is shifting imperceptibly with the water, ever aware of its surroundings.

Over against the other bank, where water is pouring out of the sluice from the old prawn ponds into the main river, gullies and niches have been eroded into the mud, and a Water Monitor (*Varanus salvator*) rests half out on the mud. It is dull, blackish, green, speckled, inert; it has not moulted its skin for several months. It is in the shade cast by the *Avicennia* mangrove foliage as the sun warms steadily, and soon it will be basking. The overnight dew on those *Avicennia* leaves has not yet burned off, but has trickled down to form a drop at the tip of every leaf. If you touch one and put it to your tongue, it tastes very salty. With their roots constantly bathed in the sea, the trees have to get rid of the salt somehow, and they have done it by crystallizing salt out of the moisture that evaporates from their stomata, all over the surface of the leaf. The dew has dissolved it, and droplets will fall back into the water below.

***Opposite, clockwise from above left:** Separated from the mainland by Sungei Bilabong Buloh, Pulau Buloh is reserved for the wildlife, although visitors can get a glimpse from Platform 2;* Toxotes jaculatix, *the Banded Archer Fish; a small Estuarine crocodile* (Crocodylus porosus) *seen at Pasir Ris Park in 2008 was eventually removed, crocodiles that settled at the Reserve remain unmolested. Often sighted from the Main Bridge, they are a source of morbid fascination. The wheel-chair friendly Mangrove Boardwalk allows everyone to easily enjoy a closer look at majestic trees and curious creatures of the mangroves. Volunteers provide regular guided walks here.*

Past the end of the bridge, where the crocodile warning sign is, that old prawn pond seems at first to be empty, but over on the other side there is movement that resolves itself into a scattering of Redshanks (*Tringa totanus*). This group arrived a couple of days ago, but others have been passing through for several weeks, and numbers are building up. Among them are one or two Greenshanks (*Tringa nebularia*), and a Marsh Sandpiper (*Tringa stagnatilis*). None of these waders seems to have been colour-ringed or flag-marked, so we cannot tell where they have come from, but it's probably somewhere like eastern Siberia or the Arctic Circle north of Korea. One fifth of the earth's circumference away, and their journey is still not done.

Right: *An otherwise untidy tree with dull leaves, Dungun* (Heritiera littoralis) *occasionally produces a fountain of pink, velvety, bell-shaped flowers. Its timber was traditionally valued for boat building particularly by pirates as it was believed to magically stop bullets.*

Right: Dubbed the 'Panda of the Mangroves', Bakau Mata Buaya (Bruguiera hainesii) *is as rare and precious as the Giant Pandas. Globally listed as 'Critically Endangered' with only 200 known mature trees worldwide, tiny Singapore has eight of these priceless treasures!*

Mangroves

Trees with legs, trees that can snorkel, a forest where the fishes skip happily out of water, and where monster lizards prowl. Welcome to the mysterious mangroves. Growing where no tree has grown before, mangrove trees are topsy-turvy and shelter bizarre creatures often seen in no other environment. A half-way forest between dry land and the salty sea, a huge diversity of life ranges through the mangroves with the flow of the tides.

Mangrove mud, black and stinking, often turns off the first-time visitor. This, however, is more a sign of life than of death and decay. Mangrove mud consists of very fine particles and is well compacted, thus poor in oxygen. But mangrove mud is rich in tiny bits of decaying plants and animals (which we politely call detritus). Special bacteria thrive here; they can breathe both with and without oxygen. At first, they use up all the oxygen. Then they start to use sulphur, releasing hydrogen sulphide as a by-product. Hydrogen sulphide turns things black and smells of rotten eggs – hence the black and stinking mud. These bacteria are in turn eaten by tiny animals and thus support food chains in the mangroves and beyond. The richness of the detritus in the mud means that there is far more carbon stored in the mud than there is in the growing trees, so mangrove mud is also an important resource in managing climate change.

How deep is the mud? At Mandai mangroves on the north coast of mainland Singapore, one of the best studied sites with some 50 scientific publications concerning a mere 18 ha (44 acres) of mangrove habitat, it is some 14–16 m (46–52 ft) from the mud surface down to the bedrock. There must be some three million cubic m (106 million cubic ft) of mud at this site alone. Only when disturbed does the mud cause trouble: dug out and left to dry onshore, sulphides oxidize to form acid sulphates, damaging to fisheries.

Snorkelling trees

It's tough to stay upright growing in soft, oxygen-poor mud, and at the same time coping with tidal changes twice a day. The various types of mangrove tree have developed a range of methods to overcome the softness of the mud, the shortage of oxygen and the frequent changes of tide. *Avicennia* trees snorkel through air-breathing roots that grow upwards from the ground. Called pneumatophores, these pencil-shaped roots emerge laterally from shallow horizontal roots just below the surface of the mud. A 3-m (10-ft) tall *Avicennia* can have 10,000 pneumatophores. Like massive, lumbering, many-limbed creatures, *Rhizophora* trees grow roots that step long distances above the mud surface. These aerial roots may form leg-like stilts for the tree, while additional prop roots grow vertically downwards from the branches to further stabilize the tree. Getting down and comfortable in the mud, *Bruguiera* has its knee roots tucked up around it. These are underground roots that emerge from the mud and then loop back downwards, often with a knobbly bump at the highest point of the loop that resembles a knee. The stately and thick trunked *Xylocarpus* produces flat, sinuous plank roots that act as buttresses to the tall trees.

All these aerial roots have special tiny pores (lenticels) to take in air that is stored in large air spaces in the roots. Much like a diver's air tanks, these air spaces – sometimes up to 40 per cent of the root's volume – provide oxygen to the tree during high tide when most or all of the aerial roots may be submerged. Respiration by the tree changes the relative concentrations of the various gases (especially oxygen and carbon dioxide) in this stored air, and the changes in their partial pressures then act as a pumping mechanism. 'Normal' roots for absorbing nutrients are tiny and emerge near the muddy surface. The architecture of the mangroves, with props, aerators, anchors, cables and absorbers of gases and nutrients, is a wonderful demonstration of the integration of many functions into one diversified system. Within these roots oxygen is indeed necessary for growth in the anoxic mud, and while the leaves of the tree are absorbing carbon dioxide for breakdown to provide oxygen internally to the tissues, and then releasing oxygen after use, in the pneumatophores the oxygen can be taken in directly.

With their strange root structures, mangrove forests stabilize both themselves and the soft shore they grow in against tidal and river currents, and reduce the erosion that might happen during violent storms. Along the southern and western shores of

Right: Api-api Putih (Avicennia alba) *is common in Singapore mangroves, with its distinctive pencil-like roots and tiny yellow flowers held in a cross-like formation.*

*Opposite: Icons of the mangroves, Bakau (*Rhizophora *spp.) stand on arching stilt roots and have dangling prop roots. They are common, sometimes growing so densely in Singapore that they form an impenetrable 'fence' of interlocking stilt roots taller than a man.*

Left: In the gloomy mangrove forest, the 'flowers' of Tumu (Bruguiera gymnorrhiza) provide a startling splash of colour. The red waxy calyx encloses delicate petals that hold loose pollen under tension. When probed at the base, the petal explosively unzips to anoint the visiting pollinator with pollen.

Below: Nyireh (Xylocarpus rumphii) is the rarest of the genus, with fewer than 10 known mature trees in Singapore. Growing beneath natural rocky cliffs and in undisturbed mangroves, it has glossy, green, heart-shaped leaves with golden veins and fruits that resemble big green apples.

Singapore these will often be early morning Sumatra storm fronts rolling in from Indonesia, hitting some of the remaining mangrove patches on the mainland such as Berlayar Creek and the Pandan River. During the northeast monsoon, winds from the direction of the South China Sea are more likely, and detailed calculations have shown the link between wind speeds at different distances between Borneo and Vietnam, and the timing and height of tides reaching Singapore some hours later. If storms coincide with a high tide, the role of the mangroves becomes even more important in ameliorating storm surges.

Above: The Pasir Ris mangrove boardwalk lies in the heart of dense public housing. Nevertheless, visitors can enjoy viewing nesting herons, water monitors, mudskippers and more. A family of Smooth Otters (Lutrogale perspicillata) *visits regularly and it is the only mainland site for sightings of the rare Mangrove Pitta* (Pitta megarhyncha). *It is also home to some uncommon native mangrove trees such as* Bruguiera parviflora *and* Rhizophora stylosa.

Salty solutions

Having to extract pure water from the sea makes mangrove trees, literally, nature's desalination plants. All mangrove trees exclude most of the salt in seawater at the root level – their first level of defence – but some have more effective ultrafiltration in the roots to exclude even more salt. A few can tolerate high levels of salt in their tissues, secreting the excess salt on their leaves, which glitter in hot weather with an encrustation of salt. Mangrove trees protect the hard-won pure water in their tissues much as desert plants do. Water may be stored in succulent leaves. To reduce water loss, leaves may be woolly or thick and waxy. Leaf-eating insects are deterred by spiny or waxy leaves, and by high levels of tannins and other toxins. Though Singapore's mangroves are now too restricted to support an industry, such tannins were once used in South-East Asia for the treatment and preservation of leather and other goods. Mangroves also yield timber, seafood, and even honey.

If it's hard for adult trees to cope with their environment, it's even tougher for tender seedlings that are usually dispersed by seawater. Thus many mangrove mother trees give their offspring a special head start. In some mangrove species, the fruit does not fall away when it ripens. Instead, the seed within the fruit starts to germinate while it is still on the mother tree which continues to channel nutrients to the growing seedling. *Rhizophora* and *Bruguiera* are often festooned with hanging long 'beans', which are seedlings (more properly called propagules) hanging from the mother tree. These are already coloured a brilliant green with chlorophyll, and are photosynthesizing as well as continuing to draw on the parent tree for nutrients. When the seedling finally falls, it floats away and drifts with the tide. Some can survive for long periods at sea. When they hit land, the seedlings haul themselves upright by growth of new roots and then sprout leaves. The long stem that had already developed while they were hanging on the parent tree gives these seedlings a short-cut to sunlight, as well as to oxygen and carbon dioxide as they are often completely submerged at high tide. Amazingly, in the most extreme cases young seedlings can survive being completely underwater until they are big enough to grow air-breathing roots, at about one to two years old.

In some plants, the growing seed does not break through the fruit wall while the seed is on the mother plant but only after the fruit falls off. This is the case with *Avicennia* and the seed coat of its fruits drops away more quickly in water of the right warmth and salinity, usually in a spot best suited for an *Avicennia* seedling.

Above: Api-api Jambu (Avicennia marina) *is 'Critically Endangered' in Singapore with fewer than 20 trees. Surprisingly, many of these trees are found on Pulau Semakau, located next to Singapore's only landfill.*

Vertical Highway

The vertical scaffoldings of aerial roots are life-saving highways for small creatures needing to escape fishy predators that swarm with each incoming tide. In the fast lane, tree-climbing crabs scuttle high up, then scramble back down to forage on the mud at low tide. In the slow lane, snails creep up, starting well before the tide turns to make up for their lack of speed. Road-hogging mudskippers cling to the roots at high tide but near the waterline. The tangle of roots provides a surface for all kinds of creatures to settle on, from algae to shellfish.

A mangrove tree may be full of clams, not only on its roots, but even among its leaves. Leaf Oysters (*Isognomon ephippium*) often lie scattered like large silvery coins among mangrove roots. Mangrove Jingle Clams (*Enigmonia aenigmatica*) may stud leaves and tree trunks like shiny scales. Their delicate thin shells with a rainbow sheen have two valves. One valve is flatter, with a notch or hole through which the animal secretes byssus threads to adhere to the surface of the branch or trunk. The other valve is usually slightly conical in shape.

Contrary to popular fears, mangrove trees are not draped in countless dangerous snakes. In fact, it requires patient observation to spot one. The Shore or Mangrove Pit Viper (*Cryptelytrops purpureomaculatus*) looks just like another tree branch as it coils. The most common snake in Singapore's mangroves is the endearing and harmless Dog-faced Watersnake (*Cerberus rynchops*). At dusk, large numbers emerge on the mudflats and pools to hunt small fishes.

Countless filter feeders on the aerial roots make the mangroves a natural net, so that clearer water washes out into the sea, allowing coral reefs to flourish nearby. Mangroves are also an important nursery for young fishes and shrimps that will move out to deeper waters as they grow up. In the sunlit penthouse layer of the mangrove forest, branches provide nesting sites for large herons and another world of specialized epiphytes that never touch the mud or sea.

*Left: Like giant flattened spiders, Tree Climbing Crabs (*Episesarma spp.) clamber in mangrove trees. At high tide during the day, they cling to trees just above the water line, probably to avoid both aquatic predators, as well as airborne ones such as birds. At night they may climb higher to forage on leaves. Many* Episesarma *species are burrowers, digging tunnels in mud lobster mounds.*

Landward and seaward edges

A curious moonscape of tall mud mounds can be found in the back mangroves, the landward region of the mangrove forest. Created by mud lobsters (*Thalassina* spp.), this is a critical habitat that enriches the biodiversity of a mangrove. Almost never seen in the open, the mud lobster lives deep underground in a U-shaped tunnel. Growing up to 30 cm (12 in) long, it is not a true lobster but more of a giant shrimp. It is believed to eat mud and digest the rich organic remains within it. As it eats-and-digs, it recycles nutrients from deep underground, bringing these within reach of other plants and animals. Its digging also aerates the otherwise oxygen-poor ground.

Unheeded by the mud lobster, all this digging eventually results in a mound that is typically less than 1 m (3 ft 3 in) but can reach 2 m (6 ft 6 in) in height. This mud lobster 'condominium' is a perfect home for other animals, its surface being drier and harder than the surroundings. Dwellers on and in

the mound can include snakes, crabs, ants, spiders, worms, clams and shrimps. These create their own burrows leading inwards from the surface of the mound, in contrast to the mud lobster throwing mud outwards. Some can seal their burrow openings against the occasional high spring tide. Others have tall chimneys. Some animals are confined only to mud lobster mounds. These include the Hairy-foot Mangrove Spider (*Idioctis littoralis*) that was first described from Singapore. Some plants also appear to grow better on these mounds than on the adjacent mud and soil. The mud lobster condominium comes complete with indoor swimming pool; water trapped inside the mound system forms pools that shelter various small aquatic animals at low tide.

On the seaward side of some Singapore mangroves, soft, liquid mud forms extensive flats. Thick with food particles from the mangrove trees, this perennially wet and squishy habitat is great for burrowing marine life. Riddled with countless worms, clams and other succulent creatures, mudflats are rich feeding grounds

Above: **S**trange 'volcanoes' in the mangroves are created by mud lobsters. This unique and rich ecosystem is now rare in Singapore as much of the back mangroves have been developed.

Top: The mud lobster (Thalassina *spp.*) is rarely seen above ground. Mud lobsters play a critical role and are considered a keystone species for a healthy back mangrove.

Above: This large bumpy-bodied sea anemone is commonly seen on Singapore's mudflats, but is so new to science that it has yet to be named. It was among the many finds during Singapore's first Comprehensive Marine Biodiversity Survey.

for animals that can forage there. Chief among them are shorebirds that daintily probe the mudflats as their long-toed feet keep them from sinking. On Singapore shores the commonest migrants are Whimbrels *(Numenius phaeopus)*, Redshanks *(Tringa totanus)*, Greenshanks *(Tringa nebularia)* and other sandpipers and plovers. Much like human fast-food joints, mudflats and other wetlands are critical stopovers for migratory birds to rest and refuel on high-energy food that can be harvested quickly. A chain of such wetland stopovers forms a flyway. Singapore is part of the East Asian-Australasian Flyway. Often, migratory birds must fly non-stop between such stopovers as there may be no suitable habitats for them in between. The destruction of intermediate stepping stones can affect the continued existence of these marvellous birds by making the distances from one suitable spot to the next just too long. As shorebirds feed, they also give back to the health of the shore: studies have shown that shorebird droppings help to heal damaged seagrass meadows.

Right: Of ancient lineage from before the dinosaurs, the Mangrove Horseshoe Crab (Carcinoscorpius rotundicauda) *is still abundant in Singapore. Often seen in pairs, the smaller male hitches onto the back of a female with special hooked claws. Another species, the Coastal Horseshoe Crab* (Tachypleus gigas) *is also regularly seen.*

No durians without mangroves?

Durians are dearly loved by many local people, almost to the point of obsession. Many are surprised to learn that mangroves have a critical role in ensuring a continuing supply of this much loved fruit, although the fruit orchards can be far inland. Durians have fluffy white night-blooming flowers that are pollinated by bats that feed only on pollen and nectar. A study in Peninsular Malaysia found that durian flowers are pollinated almost entirely by a single species of bat, the Cave Nectar Bat (*Eonycteris spelaea*), and a study in Thailand found that each blossom is visited on average 26 times per night, implying quick replenishment of its nectar to encourage repeat visits. These nectar-feeding bats roost primarily in limestone caves, but also in old buildings, under bridges and in crevices in rockfaces. Now scarce in Singapore, they are fast flyers that forage up to a 50-km (30-mile) radius from their roost site each night in search of pollen and nectar from a wide variety of plants. Durians bloom only once or twice a year, and thus cannot be the primary source of food for these bats. Indeed, the study found that the bats' range includes mangroves with *Sonneratia* species, which also have fluffy white night-blooming flowers. It was found that mangrove trees, especially *Sonneratia alba*, are important sources of food for these bats. Thus, without mangroves, there would not be a population of these bats that also pollinate durians and other favourite fruits.

Below: *Perepat* (Sonneratia alba) *is common in Singapore's mangroves and regularly produces fluffy, white, night-blooming flowers. These may support populations of nectar-feeding bats that in turn pollinate durians and other fruits beloved by many Singaporeans.*

Islands in the use of man

An example of a successful compromise between Singapore's urban needs and the conservation of marine biodiversity, Pulau Semakau is the location of Singapore's only still functioning landfill. In 1999, when space for the last remaining landfill on Singapore's mainland was exhausted, the Semakau Landfill was created by enclosing 350 ha (865 acres) of shallow sea within a 7-km (4.3-mile) long rock bund. Although half of Pulau Semakau's reefs and the whole of Pulau Sakeng, a small adjacent island, were lost in the process, vast stretches of Pulau Semakau's natural mangroves, seagrass meadows and coral reefs were spared. During the construction of the landfill, efforts were made to protect the marine ecosystem, especially mangroves and corals. Two large patches of mangrove were replanted to replace those removed during construction of the bund. Wildlife continues to thrive on Pulau Semakau, and the air and water quality remains good.

Pulau Semakau's enormous intertidal shores are rich in amazing wildlife. The natural mangroves there shelter a wide variety of plants and animals, many no longer seen on the mainland or on other islands. Recent sightings include Peregrine Falcons (*Falco peregrinus*) and Smooth-coated Otters (*Lutrogale perspicillata*), and several locally rare or endangered plants are found on the undisturbed part of the island. The vast seagrass meadow off the west coast, possibly the largest in Singapore, has seven species of seagrasses and is the location of the seagrass species most recently rediscovered in Singapore: *Halophila decipiens*. A wide zone of reef flats leads to coral reefs that shelter a good range of hard corals and associated reef life. Sea turtles and dolphins are often sighted in the waters off Pulau Semakau. Flanking Pulau Semakau are the last of the large submerged reefs in

Above: Flaring at the refineries on Pulau Bukom regularly occurs close to the mangroves and shores of Pulau Semakau.

Singapore: Terumbu Semakau, Terumbu Raya, Beting Bemban Besar and Beting Besar.

Since 2005 members of the public have been encouraged to visit Pulau Semakau for intertidal walks, bird watching, sport fishing, star gazing and other nature-related recreational activities. This is often integrated with a tour of the landfill operations. Visitors who are stunned by the amazing wildlife seen on Pulau Semakau are also immediately reminded of how daily urban life directly impacts Singapore's natural spaces. Tour participants often leave with renewed determination to reduce waste, to reuse and recycle.

On the other side of the nation, Pulau Ubin supports the last 'kampung' or traditional village in Singapore, the last offshore island with a residential population who still live off the land. A stroll through Pulau Ubin takes you back to the Singapore of the 1960s with the simpler pleasures of life, as easy on the soul as the pocket book. For a few dollars, visitors can spend a day in the slow lane, walking or cycling along rustic roads beneath the swaying coconut palms, exploring shady trails in overgrown rubber plantations, enjoying panoramic views over the disused granite quarries that were the source for the construction of Horsburgh Lighthouse, now taken over by colonies of Grey Herons (*Ardea cinerea*), and checking out the secluded beaches and flourishing mangroves. Among the special features is a Sensory Trail designed for the visually impaired, which encourages visitors to experience nature with all their senses; a much needed refresher for jaded urbanites too.

Chek Jawa is among the best-known destinations on Pulau Ubin. It became famous when plans to reclaim it were deferred in 2001, an unusual U-turn in development decisions. Encompassing six beautiful ecosystems now rare on the mainland, Chek Jawa is easily explored by a boardwalk that was completed in 2007. It provides an easy introduction, even for young children, to the mysterious world of mangroves and to Singapore's last extensive coastal forests. Low-tide walks allow a closer look at the intertidal zone

Above: When the Semakau Landfill was built in 1999, two large patches of mangrove were replanted to replace those removed during construction. Since then, mangrove seedlings have started to settle naturally among and beyond the replanted mangroves, improving the species richness and expanding the area.

Opposite: Terumbu Bemban has portions of rich reefs, as do some of the 10 other large submerged reef flats that still remain relatively untouched. Most of these are near the Semakau Landfill and refineries on Pulau Bukom.

of rocky shores, seagrass meadows, sand flats and reef flats. From a newly constructed tower, there is a breathtaking view across the forest, mangroves and sea stretching to the mountains of Johor in Malaysia.

The shores of Pulau Ubin and particularly Chek Jawa are among the last bastions of increasingly rare estuarine and marine life in the Johor Straits. Nearby Pulau Tekong, which is restricted to military use, has been extensively affected by reclamation, while few mainland shores in the Johor Straits have escaped development. Each of the mangrove-dominated parts of these islands has retained a selection of mangrove birds. Pulau Tekong mangroves are now characterized by the Black-naped Monarch (*Hypothymis azurea*), Mangrove Blue Flycatcher (*Cyornis rufigastra*) and the globally threatened Mangrove Pitta (*Pitta megarhyncha*), but for all of these there are occasional records from other islands or from the Singapore mainland. Pulau Ubin was the site first recolonized (in 1997) by Oriental Pied Hornbills (*Anthracoceros albirostris*) from the nearby

Malaysian mangrove coast, a bird that has been the subject of detailed studies – its willingness to breed in artificial nestboxes has allowed scientists to film and study its behaviour within the nest. Because small islands have small populations, interchange between islands must occur. So it is strategic to conserve clusters such as the Southern Islands, or Pulau Ubin, Tekong and Pasir Ris.

Above: Chek Jawa on Pulau Ubin is one of Singapore's few remaining shores with a complete spectrum of natural ecosystems from coastal forest, mangroves, mudflats, sandy shores, seagrass meadows to a reefy edge. Visitors can easily explore some of these along a 1km boardwalk.

Opposite: Internationally threatened, the Mangrove Pitta (Pitta megarhyncha) *is virtually confined to mangroves; known from the islands Pulau Ubin and Pulau Tekong, it has recently been seen on mainland Singapore which may suggest population exchange.*

Left: Smooth Otters (Lutrogale perspicillata) *are encountered more often than might be expected in such a highly urbanized island. These delightful creatures are regularly seen at Sungei Buloh Wetland Reserve where they have grown accustomed to people and will happily play, feed and rest in plain view. They have also been spotted at Pasir Ris, Pulau Ubin and even at the quieter stretches of Changi Beach. One seems to have settled at Pulau Semakau.*

Left: Mudskippers display aggressively with their large colourful dorsal fins. Previously mistaken for juvenile Giant Mudskippers, these Yellow-spotted Mudskippers (Periophthalmus walailakae) were only described in 2002 although they are common in Singapore's mangroves.

Mischevious mudskippers

Mudskippers are among the most boisterous creatures seen on the mudflats at low tide, fish that emerge from the water and shuffle and hop across the mud. Often mistaken for amphibians or reptiles, they nevertheless breathe with gills. Just as scuba divers bring tanks of air underwater, mudskippers bring little tanks of water in their gills so they can wander about briefly on land. They can also absorb oxygen through their wet skin. This gives them a huge advantage over water-bound creatures, and mudskippers are the only fishes to rule the mudflats at low tide. They can also leap up onto tree roots and trunks, clinging on with modified sucker-like fins beneath the body. While some frantically renovate burrows in the mud before the tide returns, others spend their time feeding. The more quarrelsome males chase one another, defending an area around their burrow and communicating by raising their large, colourful dorsal fins.

Above: The largest species, the Giant Mudskipper (Periophthalmodon schlosseri) *is often seen near its personal 'swimming pool'. This neat circular pool is the entrance to the underground nursery for its young. The fish laboriously digs out deep tunnels using only its mouth, spitting out balls of mud around the pool. Each male defends his pool, returning to it periodically for a fresh gulp of water.*

Low tide is also a time to attract a mate. The long, almost snake-like Bearded Mudskipper (*Scartelaos histophorus*) performs a stunning feat to impress the ladies. It leaps 'on the spot', repeatedly hurling itself almost vertically, briefly standing on its tail while spreading out its pectoral fins. When not leaping, it communicates by raising its elegant, tall, first dorsal fin.

The largest of them, the Giant Mudskipper (*Periophthalmodon schlosseri*), is often seen in or near its personal swimming pool, a large circular pool of water with neat walls. This is the entrance to deep tunnels in the mud which act as a nursery for its young. The fish laboriously builds its mud mansion using only its mouth. A handsome fish with black stripes, the Giant Mudskipper aggressively hunts prawns, small crabs and insects. It may even snack on smaller mudskippers.

One of the prettiest species is the Blue-spotted Mudskipper (*Boleophthalmus boddarti*), boldly barred with electric blue spots all over its body, and with a beautiful signalling dorsal fin that bears delicate terminal filaments. This mudskipper grazes on edible titbits on the surface of the mud, gathering these by moving its head from side to side.

Curious mangrove crabs

An otherwise drab creature, the Face-banded Sesarmine Crab (*Perisesarma* spp.) has a bright green or blue band across its face and red or dark claws. These startling colours are presumably most easily seen by another crab and probably play a part in mating rituals or male rivalry. Commonly seen in some of Singapore's mangroves, the various *Perisesarma* species can make up significant biomass among mangrove crabs and play an important ecological role. As they feed on mangrove leaves, nutrients in the mangrove forest are quickly recycled.

Tree-climbing crabs (*Episesarma* spp.) clamber like giant flattened spiders up and down the

Above: *The male fiddler crab (Uca spp.) waves its one huge brightly coloured pincer to attract a mate.*

Left: *The almost snake-like Bearded Mudskipper (Scartelaos histophorus) performs a stunning dance to impress the ladies. It leaps 'on the spot', repeatedly hurling itself almost vertically, briefly standing on its tail while spreading out its pectoral fins.*

Above: The Face-banded Sesarmine Crab (Perisesarma spp.) has brightly coloured claws and band across the face that may be used in mating rituals or male rivalry.

mangrove trees. Able to stay out of water for some time, they eat mainly mangrove leaves and may also scavenge dead animals. At high tide during the day, they cling to tree trunks just above the water line and remain motionless. They probably do this to avoid both aquatic predators in the water, as well as airborne predators such as birds. At night they may climb higher, up to 6 m (20 ft), into the crowns of the trees to forage on leaves. They also gather leaves from the ground. Many other species of *Episesarma* are burrowers, digging holes at the base of mangrove trees and in mud lobster mounds.

A variety of colourful tiny fiddler crabs (*Uca* spp.) can be seen in the back mangroves, often living in burrows with chimneys. These are among the most famous of mangrove creatures, renowned for the single big signalling claw that each male possesses. This is too small to fend off predators and too large for feeding on fine particles found in sand; he uses his other tiny feeding pincer for this. Instead, the strikingly coloured pincer is used to attract females, each male waving it in a rhythm unique to his species, a crustacean's version of serenading on a violin.

Some serpents

Contrary to popular fears, mangrove trees are not draped in countless dangerous snakes. In fact, it requires patient observation to spot one. The Shore or Mangrove Pit Viper (*Cryptelytrops purpureomaculatus*) looks just like another slender tree branch as it coils motionless among trees and bushes. A rather angry looking snake with red eyes on a broad triangular head, it has a prehensile tail that can grip a branch when it lunges out for a lethal bite. This venomous snake can strike far and rapidly and can be aggressive. But like most snakes, it will not harm if left undisturbed.

The most common snake in Singapore's mangroves is the rather endearing and harmless Dog-faced Watersnake (*Cerberus rynchops*). At dusk, large numbers emerge from mud burrows and hiding places to hunt fish.

Singapore's mangroves are unusual in several ways, some of them due to man's influence. They

Above: Water Monitors (Varanus salvator) can be abundant on mangrove coasts and islands, and swim long distances. Mainly scavengers, they seem to obtain their fresh water needs from their food such as live or dead fish, frogs and molluscs. When not hunted they can grow very large – more than 2 m (6 ft) long – and are indifferent to humans.

have never been harvested on rotation for timber, in the way that has been practised through much of South-East Asia. This means that stands of single-age trees all planted at the same time at a uniform density are not normal in Singapore. In places ancient trees have survived because of the lack of local harvesting. *Sonneratia alba* trees at Pulau Pawai are a superb example of this, with the oldest trees on the mudflats of the south coast resting on huge boughs that have settled onto the surface, and arrays of pneumatophores spreading up to a 22-m (72-ft) radius around each tree.

In addition, Singapore has some hard-to-identify mangrove trees. One of these is *Ceriops zippeliana*, only described with certainty in Singapore in 2009. It actually seems commoner than the species with which it had been confused, *Ceriops tagal*.

A third oddity of Singapore's mangroves is the presence of lateritic red rubble, nodules of hard rock making up the bulk of the substrate at some sites like the north coast of Pulau Tekong. Furthermore,

Singapore is renowned among the cognoscenti of algae for the accumulation of a brilliant green carpet of algae trapped among the mangrove roots. This does happen elsewhere, but not on long mainland coasts such as the Malacca Straits, and seldom to the degree found in Singapore.

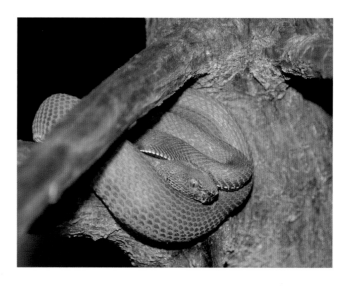

Above: With angry red eyes in a perpetual frown, the Shore or Mangrove Pit Viper (Cryptelytrops purpureomaculatus) *can grip onto a branch with its prehensile tail as it whips out for a lethal, rapid strike. This venomous predator can be aggressive, but like most snakes, is harmless if left undisturbed.*

Left: The Dog-faced Watersnake (Cerberus rynchops) *can be abundant in Singapore's mangroves. It hunts and swallows fish, including alarmingly large ones, whole. The snake has unusual protruding eyes that may be the reason for its common name.*

5

The Lowland and Coastal Hill Forest

So complex is the lowland rain forest that there is always something of interest to be seen, whether it is the strangely shaped fruit of a tree or the flight of a lizard from trunk to trunk. The forest is filled with sounds, from the birds and insects, and from the movement of the vegetation in the gentle breeze. Briefly, the songs of cicadas can drown out all other sounds. Against this background, animals go about their daily lives seeking food and shelter. Boardwalks and canopy towers within the Nature Reserves enable Singaporeans to view these events in comfort and safety.

Left: Lowland tropical evergreen rain forest contains a great variety of plant species, and is structurally very complex, with trees large and small, palms, climbers and epiphytes.

Bukit Timah: primary forest in the core of mainland Singapore

It is the tops of the trees that first begin to whisper in the wind. Initially they do so intermittently, a light flutter moving over the skin of the forest. But as the wind strengthens, it becomes more constant, and the sound builds up into a steady rustle. Then the wind begins to penetrate further down into the structure of the forest. The really big trees are too massive to sway visibly, but certainly their branches begin to heave.

There is a crackle of light, followed half a minute later by a sharp bang of thunder. The sky has darkened quickly and suddenly the wind, that was warm, has become markedly colder; it must have dropped five degrees in five minutes. What was a whisper, then a rustle, now becomes a powerful rush and boom. The yellower of the leaves above are starting to spiral down. Within the sound of the wind comes another, softer but still perceptible, as big, fat drops of rain start to fall. A third wave of sound approaches as the main storm arrives – pounding drops that begin to strip green leaves from the canopy, some singly and some in bunches still attached to the twigs that fall.

The aroma is remarkable. The rain releases all sorts of chemicals from the leaf litter and the soil. Fungi start expanding in the welcome downpour, and even the bacteria begin multiplying within minutes.

Anyone in the forest will be soaked, drenched, saturated by water. Every animal, every bird, every insect is silent. The first intense rain begins to moderate into a steady fall, then after half an hour it has eased, perhaps stopped. It is hard to tell because the foliage above is soaked, and drops will continue to fall for several hours after the rain has passed.

After the storm

The afternoon sky lightens, a thrush-like White-rumped Shama (*Copsychus malabaricus*) begins to sing, and it seems as though the forest stretches and inhales once more. As the sun comes out, a Flying Lizard (*Draco sumatranus*), that

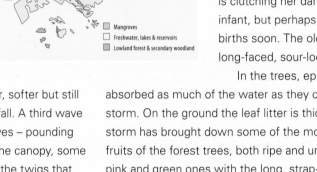

Mangroves
Freshwater, lakes & reservoirs
Lowland forest & secondary woodland

had been sheltering on the underside of a big branch, moves onto the trunk of a large tree and flashes his yellow throat-flap as a signal to others. A female comes down an adjacent tree in short hesitant runs broken by periods of stillness, then moves warily onto the forest floor and begins to dig a hole in the newly softened earth in which to lay her eggs.

In the densest part of the tree crowns a group of Long-tailed Macaques (*Macaca fascicularis*) that had been miserably soaked in their partial shelter still look disgruntled as they begin to move about in search of food. Nine or ten individuals make this rather a small troop; only one mother is clutching her dark-haired, pink-faced infant, but perhaps there will be other births soon. The old male is rather long-faced, sour-looking and irritable.

In the trees, epiphytic ferns have absorbed as much of the water as they can, till the next storm. On the ground the leaf litter is thick and wet. The storm has brought down some of the more loosely attached fruits of the forest trees, both ripe and unripe. The unripe pink and green ones with the long, strap-like, soft wings belong to a dipterocarp. There is a ripe one; it has turned brown and the wings have hardened in an elegant curve. Storms send them spinning like descending helicopters through the forest. If the fruit is left amongst the wet leaf

Opposite, clockwise from top left: *Long-tailed Macaques are amongst the dispersers of seeds in the rain forest; soft colourful stipules of the giant forest tree Keruing Belimbing* (Dipterocarpus grandiflorus) *fall to the ground after they have done their job of protecting the newly growing leaf bud, and will soon decay amongst the leaf litter; the fruits of the middle storey Menasi* (Pouteria obovata) *provide food for a variety of forest mammals and birds, and grow in a position where they can easily be reached; the Birds' Nest Fern* (Asplenium nidus) *is one of the larger and more spectacular epiphytes commonly seen in the forest.*

litter, assuming the beetles and fungi do not attack it, or it is not crushed by a foot or a falling branch, it will germinate and send its single pale root down into the earth, and its single stem will start to struggle upwards towards the light. It may have many metres of growth and many years of life ahead, having to compete with its neighbours and with its overshadowing parent for root space and for light. Should it survive, it may replace one of the nearby competitors and become a great emergent tree, from whose luxuriant crown some perching bird will look out over the forest and observe the city buildings spread out into the distance, with the sea beyond.

Right: The Black-bearded Flying Dragon (Draco melanopogon) *is one of three species of flying lizards in Singapore, capable of gliding from tree to tree by extending the frill of skin along its flanks, supported by the slender ribs.*

Below: The small, typically white, cream or pale green flowers of many rain forest trees such as Leban (Vitex pinnata) *are pollinated by insects, from the minuscule thrip to the robust Carpenter Bee* (Xylocopa latipes) *shown here.*

Diversity of trees

At least 843 species of vascular plants have been recorded from Bukit Timah Nature Reserve. This represents 56 per cent of the total extant flora of Singapore, living within an area of 1.64 sq km (0.63 sq miles), of which less than half is primary forest. There are several lessons one could draw from this. One is that Bukit Timah is a gem that must be conserved at all costs. Another is the shocking loss that must have been caused by forest removal through the rest of Singapore during the period from 1819 to 1884. Yet another is the fragility of those plants in Bukit Timah, many of them (especially the big trees) with frighteningly small populations. Conversely, only three plant species that were entirely confined to Singapore have become globally extinct, and 70 per cent of the native flora has survived clearance of about 97 per cent of the native vegetation. Every year, several rediscoveries are made of plants that had been thought lost.

Small populations may be fragile, but they are the basis for breeding programmes to bolster the plant community, spread rare species back into a wider range of localities and reduce risks of extinction.

The 843 species recorded from Bukit Timah are only a part of the total forest flora. A couple of hundred species are confined to the Central Catchment Nature Reserve, and others can be located in remaining forested patches elsewhere on the mainland and on the offshore islands. Altogether, fully two-thirds of Singapore's current native flora consists of forest-adapted plants, a very interesting perspective in view of the degree of forest loss. The losses, then, have been not so much loss of species as loss of population size with respect to each of the remaining species, and loss of animal species dependent on the forest.

Above: The crowns of emergent trees, often members of the Family Dipterocarpaceae, project above the level of the main forest canopy.

Forest Ecology

If we knew the details better, we might also be impressed by the changes that have occurred in physical and chemical processes. The reduction in forest cover in Singapore must have greatly altered biomass, carbon storage above and below ground, microbial processes in the soil, primary production and nutrient capture. Some of these would have been offset by replacement of the forest with other vegetation, sometimes faster-growing. The contribution of grassland (whether self-seeded wild grasses on newly cleared land, or deliberately created turf), for example, would not be small. But the web of interactions in the native forest is vastly greater.

Most spectacular of those interactions is the mass flowering that occurs every few years in response to El Niño climatic events. Singapore's trees, especially the dipterocarps, continue to participate in these region-wide flowerings in spite of the reduction in forest area, local weather conditions, reductions in species diversity, and changes in the pollinators and seed predators. Litter disturbance and disturbance of the soil surface by animals loosen it up and make a significant difference to the density of successful germination, though overall germination rates can be very low, perhaps only one-twentieth of those seeds available on the forest floor.

Dipterocarp trees (trees of the Family Dipterocarpaceae named for their robust two-winged fruits, and a favoured source of timber throughout the South-East Asian forests) typically dominate the main canopy and the emergent layers of the forest. The fact that they are the most enthusiastic participants in mass flowering makes them very conspicuous in certain years, but rare species can easily be overlooked in the intervening

Above: The delicate multipinnate fronds of tree-ferns, and the more substantial glossy fronds and fishtails of climbing palms add to the great diversity of foliage shapes in the middle and lower storey of the forest; at a treefall gap they take advantage of the brilliant sunlight.

Right: A few understorey trees such as wild Tampoi (Baccaurea spp.) *carry fruits attractive to arboreal mammals all the way up their trunks, and signal their presence with bright colours; even some frugivorous birds can snap up these fruits while in flight.*

flowerless years. In 2005 a small cluster of the massive *Dipterocarpus tempehes* was discovered in the central nature reserves, only because the fruits were noticeably different from any seen by local botanists previously. This tree was previously known only from Borneo, but it is remarkable that in 2005 the same species was also discovered for the first time in Peninsular Malaysia, also through observation of the fruits. Because of their commercial importance, dipterocarps have been studied closely for many decades, yet not a single botanist or forester had found *Dipterocarpus tempehes* before, and despite the fact that the forests of Singapore and Peninsular Malaysia have been much more intensely studied than those of Borneo. Does this mean that *Dipterocarpus tempehes* flowered and fruited but went unnoticed in 1997, 1994, 1982–83, 1976, 1968, 1963, and during all those earlier mass flowerings, or does it mean that the trees had been standing there, fruitless, decade after decade, waiting for just the right conditions?

Just as elsewhere in the tropics, the forest contains many tree species, each one of which occurs at very low density. This means wide gaps between individual specimens of a given tree, and little clue as to why a particular tree successfully germinated and established itself at a given spot. Was it chance that the uneaten fruit happened to land in that spot and that anywhere else would have been just as good, or did viable seeds fall in many places and only that particular spot offered just the right conditions? Drought tolerance by germinating seeds and newly established seedlings is thought to be one of the important factors affecting the microhabitat selection of sites often seen among the forest tree species. Young seedlings can respond in varied ways

Above: The young leaves of forest trees in the tropics are often brightly coloured, red, orange or even white, and are as limp as tissue. Their physical and chemical characteristics are thought to be defences against ultraviolet light and herbivorous insects.

to water stress. Seedlings of various species show a reduction in total leaf area when grown under water stress, an increase in leaf mass per unit area, and an increased allocation of tissue resources towards the making of fine lateral rootlets. Proper functioning of the water transport system within the seedling, evapotranspiration and transport of nutrients depend on maintaining adequate water potential at the growing tips. Different species vary in their ability to do so when placed under regimes in which differing amounts of water are supplied, and the duration of a simulated drought. Even though closely related, different genera, such as *Hopea* and *Vatica* among the dipterocarps, can show divergent responses and probably the same applies to different species within a single genus.

Singapore has one of the world's most equable climates, with minimal variation from month to month. Singapore also has one of the world's highest rates of lightning strikes; past records, when mapped, show a vulnerable swathe from near the city in the southern centre of the island, extending northwest through to Lim Chu Kang. Big trees are particularly susceptible to lightning strike. The whole crown of a 36-m (118-ft) tall *Anisoptera megistocarpa* in the Botanic Gardens Jungle was snapped off two-thirds of the way up the trunk by a single stroke of lightning in 1964. Again the scale of Singapore comes into play, for where the area of forest is small and the number of big trees is limited, the relative impact of such an incident can be great. The death and subsequent fall of a single forest giant in a tiny forest patch can alter the whole character and fortunes of the vegetation in a way that would never occur if a similar tree were to be struck by lightning in a huge mainland forest.

One striking event in February 2011 was a brief but violent storm over Mandai forest, in the northern part of the Central Catchment Nature Reserve. A sudden downdraught beginning over one of the reservoirs knocked over many trees across several tens of hectares. Whether this constituted as much as 3 per cent or just 1 per cent or less of Singapore's remaining forests can be argued,

Above: *Fierce squalls caused by a downdraught of cold air that then spilt sideways through the adjacent secondary forest caused the snapping of many tree trunks above head height; these were mostly soft-timbered species such as Mahang (Macaranga gigantea).*

Opposite: *The very tall, nearly straight trunks of the forest giants made them valuable to the timber industry, but most forest in Singapore had already been converted to agricultural land long before forestry was scientifically established in the region.*

depending on the definition of forest. Whatever the figure, it represented a significant proportion of all Singapore's forests. This is not to suggest that the forest is doomed – indeed with enrichment planting the area is rapidly recovering – but it highlights the fragility of small areas and shows the importance of interventionist management in maintaining the predominantly wild, natural, native ecosystems. This must include management of large mammals such as Wild Boar that influence the forest.

Forest home for wildlife

Animal populations require management just as much as the plants, when it comes to small areas in a densely populated nation. The Long-tailed Macaque (*Macaca fascicularis*), first described and named by Stamford Raffles in 1821, has not merely persisted until today but is one of the commonest and most conspicuous of all forest mammals in the nature reserves. A census conducted in 2007 showed a population of some 1,500 Long-tailed Macaques, mostly on the mainland but including some on the outlying islands. There are documented human–wildlife conflicts in Singapore involving non-primates such as pythons and birds, but the single most common source of conflict that invariably makes the headlines involves the Long-tailed Macaque.

Before 2000 the wild population of Long-tailed Macaques, particularly those at Bukit Timah Nature Reserve, contributed much to our understanding of the ecology of the tropical rainforest with respect to seed dispersal and forest phenology. Recent research on Singapore's Long-tailed Macaques has focused on bidirectional disease transmission, human–macaque interactions and morphological variation. All these studies contributed immensely to our understanding of the ecology and taxonomy of this species.

In modern Singapore, the conflict arising from the human–macaque interface usually stems from food provisioning, both intentional and unintentional, and also intolerance and even an irrational fear of macaques. The areas where the conflicts are most severe are usually residential sites in the vicinity of the forested nature reserves, as the Long-tailed Macaques favour forest edges. The human–macaque conflict in Singapore is not a recent phenomenon but started sometime in the early 1970s when the Singapore Botanic Gardens removed groups of 'nuisance monkeys' within its boundaries. Since that episode, the Agri-Food and Veterinary Authority (AVA) has publicly stated that culling will only be a 'last resort and only if the monkeys become aggressive and pose a danger to the public' (effective April 2019, AVA was dissolved and its animal and veterinary functions

Left: There are about 1,500 Long-tailed Macaques in Singapore, mostly living within the forest and especially along the forested edges of the Nature Reserves; troops of ten to twenty individuals are common and reproductive rates are high.

Opposite: In the Central Catchment Nature Reserve, the Treetop Walk provides good opportunities to study the plant and animal life of the forest canopy. This sturdy construction is open to the public on most days.

taken under the purview of the Animal & Veterinary Service, a cluster under the National Parks Board). This is assessed using a scoring system, and so far culling has rarely been needed.

The National Parks Board has also adopted several measures to deal with human–macaque conflict in Singapore, often in co-operation with other agencies. The possibilities of translocation and sterilization have been explored in the past, but translocation is not feasible due to the lack of forested areas for release of macaques without causing further conflict. Furthermore, translocated animals might still seek out humans. Sterilization as a population control measure has been shown to be partially effective in places with commensal macaques, such as Gibraltar and Hong Kong, although there remains a question of the effect of sterilization on macaque behaviour in the long term. For the time being, agencies in Singapore favour other less drastic practices for long-term management of the macaque population including public education and outreach, relocation

Above: Long-tailed Macaques sometimes become too used to people and adult males in particular become unafraid and can make threatening displays; but sensible behaviour by members of the public minimizes conflicts.

Left: The leaf litter is carpeted with fallen blossoms of the Durian (Durio zibethinus), *that have been at their peak during the previous night when they were irresistible to pollinating bats. In a few months the ripe fruits will become a favoured food of monkeys and humans.*

of individual monkeys that have been shown to be habitual nuisances, the implementation of a total feeding ban and elimination of artificial food sources. Members of the public and non-governmental organizations have been broadly helpful in addressing the issue of conflicts.

Human–macaque conflict does exist in Singapore but it is much less serious than human–macaque interactions in others parts of the world. Research has show that human behaviour is the main cause of macaque-to-human interaction, and the challenge is to change human behaviour and habits to lessen potential conflicts in interface zones. In this same study, the majority of the interviewees argued for the conservation of macaques rather than their eradication. Coupled with the research conducted on macaques to date, this attests to the intrinsic value of Singapore's Long-tailed Macaques, and that the preservation of the species has an important place in safeguarding Singapore's natural heritage.

The Banded Leaf-monkey (*Presbytis femoralis*),

Singapore's only other wild monkey species, has required a very different approach. As described in the chapter on freshwater swamp forest (page 149), the population is now gradually recovering from a severe population bottleneck, and tree planting is used both to enrich the potential food supply and to create physical connections across forest gaps. This is a long-term strategy to encourage the population increase in a species that is benign towards humans, and to allow its expansion back into the dryland forest that it once inhabited. Such efforts are meant not only to safeguard the populations of the animals themselves, but to maintain the forest as a functioning system with pollinators, seed dispersers and nutrient recyclers all playing their part to ensure that the forest itself is sustainable.

Above: The fruits of Kembang Semangkok (Scaphium macropodum) are easily recognised by the boat-shaped bract around them; when a ripe seed is cut and placed in water it will produce a great volume of mucilage. Monkeys eat the seeds and perhaps also value this jelly.

Left: The Rusty Oilfruit (Elaeocarpus ferrugineus) is a tree whose crown is at the level of the main forest canopy, where its foliage shows a characteristic russet tone on the new leaves, on the veins of the old ones, and on the twigs.

Below: The Colugo (Galeopterus variegatus) is active by night, while by day its mottled fur helps to camouflage it against the dappled and lichen-patched trunks of the trees on which it rests.

Flight through the forest

Many other forest animals seem almost indifferent to the presence of humans, though they are naturally cautious. Did a small dragon just sail effortlessly through the air from one tree to another? No it was not a mirage brought on by the tropical heat. What you saw was a flying lizard of the genus *Draco*, and most probably the Sumatran Flying Dragon (*Draco sumatranus*). This is the most common flying lizard in Singapore's parks, gardens and nature reserves, while two closely related species, the Black-bearded Flying Dragon (*D. melanopogon*) and the spectacular Five-banded Flying Dragon (*D. quinquefasciatus*) are locally restricted to the rainforest reserves in Singapore.

The genus *Draco* shows astounding diversity in South-East Asia, with at least 15 species described so far. Apart from the flying dragons, Singapore is also home to at least four other groups of gliding vertebrates – the Colugo, a truly arboreal mammal

endemic to South-East Asia with the unfortunate misnomer of 'flying lemur'; the flying squirrels of which three species have been recorded on the mainland; the flying snakes of the genus *Chrysopelea*, and the flying geckos. Among the geckos, Kuhl's Gliding Gecko (*Ptychozoon kuhli*), which was only discovered on Pulau Tekong about a decade ago, is the most flight-efficient (or glide-efficient) compared to the Frilly Gecko (*Cosymbotus craspedotus*) and Brown's Flap-legged Gecko (*Luperosaurus browni*).

The occurrence of many gliding vertebrate species in the forests of tropical Asia is a peculiar phenomenon compared to the rainforests of Latin America or Africa. There are several schools of thought on why there are so many South-East Asian gliders, but the most probable reason seems to be the 'food desert theory'. This suggests that the predominance of the tropical hardwood trees of the Family Dipterocarpaceae in the forested landscape is responsible for driving the evolution of gliding vertebrates. The crowns of these lofty trees offer little

sustenance for leaf-eating gliders such as the Colugo and flying squirrels due to their resinous, hard-to-digest leaves. Similarly, there is a low level of insect prey for the gliding lizards and geckos due to the irregularity of flowering and fruiting cycles of the dipterocarp trees. Gliding makes sense for these groups of animals as it is more efficient to cover more ground while foraging in a 'food desert', and this strategy may inadvertently increase their chances of finding a mating partner as well. A single explanation is unlikely to hold for all these animals, because some are large, others small; some are nocturnal, others move by day. Gliders include herbivores and insect eaters. Like much else in the rain forest, complexity is the rule.

Above: Some one to two per cent of natural sunlight reaches the ground inside the primary rain forest, the rest being filtered out by the successive layers of vegetation from the canopy downwards; ground-living plants must compete for light, and take advantage of short-lived sun-flecks.

Small and important

Recent research has shown the continuing importance of Singapore's forests to invertebrate animals. A repeat of Wallace's beetle collecting forays, in the area of Dairy Farm and Bukit Timah, demonstrated that many of the larger species that he collected can no longer be found, but there are actually more species than Wallace collected because he was concentrating on specimens that had commercial value, and he overlooked (or more likely decided not to collect) many tiny species.

Another fairly well-known group contains the grasshoppers, crickets and katydids. With 170 species known from Singapore, an additional seven species new to science have been named in just two years. Open country grassland species could be widespread, and it is among the lowland forest fauna that really fascinating discoveries might still be made.

Julidan millipedes (*Thyropygus* spp.) include the biggest and heaviest invertebrates in Singapore's forests. Their appearance is striking, and their mating behaviour and genital structures are complex. They are very different from the simplest of millipede mating behaviours in which males deposit sperm packages on the ground that females may or may not choose to pick up. Julidans have a much more interventionist approach to sex. When a male mounts he will encounter resistance from the female, who tends to curl, and it is the task of the male – at which he may fail – to overcome this by clasping

using modified legs, by keeping the female's body straight, and in some species by inserting his second pair of legs into the female's mouthparts, where they secrete a clear liquid protein that presumably acts as a stimulant to mate. But before fertilization the male actively uses brush-bodies and a flagellum to remove from the female any sperm packages from a recent mating. No male can be confident that he has succeeded in fertilizing the female, unless he is the last to mate with her. So both the male and the female are able to exercise choice at different stages.

Though they spend most of their time on the ground, moving over and through the leaf litter, it is not unusual to see one of these guys on the lower part of a tree trunk, browsing among the damp bryophytes and lichens. This comes as a surprise to those who have only seen julidan millipedes in the New World, where they seem to live only on the ground.

So the remaining forests of Singapore have tremendous value in retaining a range of species of plants, animals and micro-organisms, some of

Right: The Common Sun Skink (Eutropis multifasciatus) is one of the most commonly seen reptiles in the forest, as it habitually warms itself in a sunny patch on the leaf litter, scuttling away to safety when disturbed by passers-by.

Opposite: The crowns of the forest trees provide a great variety of structures, including the vertical trunk, lateral branches, twigs, upper and lower leaf surfaces, sometimes supplemented by growth of climbers and epiphytes that provide many niches to be exploited by other plant and animal species.

them even now undescribed, as well as benefitting the community through their roles in education, recreation, buffering of the urban heat-island effect, research and commercialization, and the physical health and psychological well-being of residents. Over the years since they were first established in 1884, the number of forest reserves has declined due to land pressures and the shift to reliance on imported timber. They reached their peak in size in the 1930s, but this is only part of the story because much of the previous and currently existing secondary forest occurs outside the formally reserved areas.

With the aim of optimizing land use, efforts are now being made to reconnect the nature reserves so that populations of animals and plants are pooled. It is not clear how climate change will affect the forested nature reserves, so reconnection of fragments is one of the important tools to improve resilience in the face of increased temperatures, more variable rainfall and possibly more extreme local weather events. The most conspicuous of these efforts is the Eco-Link between Bukit Timah and Central Catchment Nature Reserves, bridging the six-lane Bukit Timah Expressway. Prior to construction it was thought necessary to invest in pre-project monitoring, so as to provide a basis for comparison when judging the effectiveness of the Eco-Link. So far, camera trapping has revealed Malayan Porcupine (*Hystrix brachyura*) and Large Indian Civet (*Viverra zibetha*), two mammals previously unknown from the nature reserves. With recent past discoveries of Lesser Mousedeer, Leopard Cat (*Prionailurus*

bengalensis), Wild Boar and Sambar Deer, it seems that a large mammal fauna typical of lowland forest is steadily being reconstructed. Time will tell how this affects seed dispersal and forest regeneration.

Above: Fruits of plant families such as the Sapindaceae *and* Euphorbiaceae, *favourite foods for small mammals and birds, have fruit walls that split and will then reveal either coloured flesh or a waxy aril round the seed, often rich in nutrients.*

Changing levels of forest protection in Singapore

Date	Number	Total area ha (acres)	Percentage of land	Designation
1886	13 reserves	4,676 (11,554)	9.0 per cent	Forest reserves
1907	8 reserves	6,033 (14,907)	11.3 per cent	Forest reserves
1930	9 reserves	6,570 (16,234)	11.7 per cent	Forest reserves
1951	5 reserves	3,419 (8,448)	5.4 per cent	Forest reserves
1991	2 reserves	2,417 (5,972)	3.8 per cent	Nature reserves
2011	4 reserves	3,347 (8,270)	4.6 per cent	Nature reserves

Opposite: Not only is there structural complexity within the shape of each tree, and in comparison between the different shapes and heights of each tree, but also a multitude of different shades of green.

Left: At the disturbed edge of the forest, close to water, the Common Parasol dragonfly (Neurothemis fluctuans) will sun itself on an exposed leaf tip and adjust the angle of its wings to gain maximum warmth.

Above: Also found in disturbed areas is the snail Quantula striata, the only snail in the world that is known to be luminescent, and abundant in and on the leaf litter. The shell is about 2.5 cm (1 in) across.

Poyan: coastal views in the extreme west

When you find a place to sit here, it's sometimes a bit uncomfortable where all the ferns have been removed, for the spiky ends are sharp and the turned red earth is a little damp. But it is worth a little discomfort for the view alone. Just 30 m (100 ft) down the slope in front of you are the waters of the Johor Straits. From this steep angle they look very blue. You can see why the ferns have been cleared away here, for this old Dicranopteris fern is very invasive. A few more weeks and it would have obscured the track. Fortunately, whoever did the cutting was careful not to touch that other fern, the one with the broad hand-shaped leaves. It's *Dipteris conjugata*, and this is one of only four patches known in Singapore. If you were to travel north up the Malay Peninsula you would find it growing in the mountains, but the closer to Singapore you come, the lower it grows, till here it is nearly at sea level. With binoculars you might be able to see patches of it growing on the equivalent sandstone bluffs across the straits in Johor. It specializes in these shifting coastal areas, where a landslide may clear new ground and its rhizomes can spread. At Labrador, along the south coast, the colony was overshadowed by the surrounding trees but drifting spores might seek out a new landslide somewhere.

There's an interesting mix of tough little trees on this slope. The one with the peeling bark, looking like a little eucalyptus tree, is a species of *Tristania*, and it is indeed in the same family as the Australian gum trees. This sort of habitat is typical: on a steep slope, often with its roots reaching down to the water if it is near a freshwater stream, but you will not find it right at the edge of the sea. That other grey-barked species, much more common, with the little hard green fruits each with a single soft spike at the tip, is *Adinandra*. It appears after the ground has been disturbed, so it can take advantage of these unstable coastal slopes in the same way that *Dipteris* does, though its fruit dispersal is very different from the chancy wind-dispersed spores of the fern. The *Rhodamnia* with the purplish-black fruits, dispersed

by birds, is another tree typical of coastal slopes, though again you can find it high in the mountains elsewhere. Its local name is mempoyan, and it would be interesting to know if that's the origin of the name for the nearby river, Sungei Poyan, now turned into Poyan reservoir. All these trees are rather small and slim, with small tough leaves, and slow-growing so they have very hard wood.

The *Rhodamnia* trees have some epiphytes on them. Apart from the bird's-nest fern, which has chosen an awkward spot from which it may fall before it reaches full size, there's a spread of narrow tongue-shaped *Drymoglossum* and *Pyrrosia* on one of the lower branches, and within this you can see the yellowy-green pseudobulbs of an orchid, probably just the common Pigeon Orchid. The tangle of climbers lower down is largely made up of one of the pitcher plants, rooted in the ground beneath. These unstable sandstones are poor in nutrients – you might have guessed it from the presence of the *Adinandra* – and the pitcher plants have found a crafty way of supplementing their diet. It must have been in vegetation something like this, perhaps on Labrador Hill near the harbour, that the botanist William Jack in 1819 first located his two new pitcher plants.

Opposite, clockwise from top left: The bark of Sea Pelawan (Tristania obovata), *a tree found near the Singapore coast, and elsewhere near rivers and in hill forest, is papery, pale and peeling; flowers in the coastal hill forest include the pretty Mempoyan* (Rhodamnia cinerea), *that grows where landslips may have created clearings where shrubs can grow up and small trees can become established; another plant of old landslips is the fern* Dipteris conjugata, *confined in Singapore to only four or five colonies on the west coast; Blue-throated Bee-eaters* (Merops viridis) *specialize in catching bees and dragonflies on the wing, and a Tropical Malayan Wasp* (Vespa tropica) *risks its life by passing close to a perched adult and a green-capped juvenile.*

Mangroves
Freshwater, lakes & reservoirs
Lowland forest & secondary woodland

The view below

This is a perspective you may not often see. The Barn Swallows (*Hirundo rustica*) are hawking far below, catching insects much too small for us to see, and the sun shines off their dark blue backs, against the brighter blue of the sea. There are Blue-throated Bee-eaters (*Merops viridis*) too, using a different hunting technique. They employ the bare twigs of some of the trees as perches, then sally out after dragonflies or the occasional bee. For them the distance across the straits is insignificant; like the spores of the *Dipteris*, the birds and the dragonflies can make the crossing in minutes. The only difference is that for the birds it is an everyday occurrence. For the spores of the fern, it is a once in a lifetime journey.

There aren't any seabirds in view at the moment, though you might have hoped for a tern or two, or a heron passing by, but there is a Collared Kingfisher (*Todirhamphus chloris*). And the calling of the bee-eaters may alert you to the other sounds: there is the constant whining of cicadas, so pervasive that you tune it out unless someone draws it to your attention. And there's another strange sound, somewhere down below. It's a hissing, rushing, seething – what to call it? It's hard to locate, but then, look, along the edge of the sea the surface is filled, absolutely filled, with the gaping, gobbling mouths of a school of fish. They are moving along the edge in shallow water, coming closer, and then they are past and the sound is fading away. Extraordinary! Unless you have heard and seen it for yourself, you would never believe that it's possible to actually listen to a group of fish more than two hundred metres away. We are privileged to have had this glimpse of the coastal forest at Poyan, where the public are normally excluded. Coastal patrols and protection of the water catchment for the reservoir are in effect conservation measures that help to protect these fragile low-nutrient slopes.

It gets very hot here, exposed to the direct sun; it is time to move on.

***Below:** Trailing to the ground, a pitcher plant* (Nepenthes rafflesiana) *sends up its curious spire of brown buds and yellow blossoms.*

***Opposite, clockwise from top left:** The Lesser Crested Tern* (Sterna bengalensis) *is one of those that can occasionally be spotted from shore-based observation points; the Kemutong* (Cratoxylum cochinchinense) *is another of the trees that shows peeling papery bark; pitcher plants such as* Nepenthes rafflesiana *are typical of scrubby areas with poor soils where growth is constrained by poor levels of nutrients that must be supplemented by digesting trapped insects; a coastal bird that nests in tree cavities, termite mounds, or burrows in sloping ground, the Collared Kingfisher* (Todirhamphus chloris) *is common throughout Singapore.*

6
Fresh Water and Freshwater Swamp Forest

Water is a resource carefully husbanded in Singapore's network of reservoirs, and is also critical to the support of the freshwater swamp forest – containing over 600 plant species of which more than 200 are confined to this habitat. The Banded Leaf-monkey, first described from Singapore in 1838, is also linked to freshwater swamp forest. Freshwater streams contain Singapore's best known examples of endemic species – small freshwater crabs – but fresh water also provides a niche for undesirable alien species, such as bullfrogs and Red-eared Sliders.

Opposite: Freshwater ecosystems in Singapore have experienced many changes, and now range from the shaded forest stream to the sun-baked canal where natural vegetation has been replaced by grassland.

Neo Tiew Lane: a stroll in the agricultural land of the north-west

As early as 1898 the forest along this side of the Kranji river estuary was included within Singapore's first generation of forest reserves. Now what is left is secondary forest along the margins of the water, with plenty of *Dillenia* and old fruit orchards, secondary growth and marshland. But with the impoundment of the Kranji dam in 1970 for water supply, this has turned into a useful conservation area. The walk from the main road, along the tarmac lane closed to traffic, makes for excellent birdwatching.

The *Albizia* trees mean that the scene is always changing. Introduced to the region long ago from eastern Indonesia, they are quick to grow and quick to die, but at their statuesque maximum size they have a lacy crown and smooth sparse limbs that provide forks that eagles like to nest in. The upper branches always attract drongos, cuckoos, bee-eaters and small birds of prey as useful perches, and insects in the foliage (mostly the caterpillars of the Three-spot Grass Yellow butterfly *Eurema blanda*) are responsible for the array of little birds: Common Loras (*Aegithina tiphia*), Pied Trillers (*Lalage nigra*), Asian Brown Flycatchers (*Muscicapa dauurica*), as well as the more substantial Black-naped Orioles (*Oriolus chinensis*). Rusty-breasted Cuckoos (*Cacomantis sepulcralis*) are tough to see, but if you know the calls, one a series of increasingly frantic notes up the scale and the other a long steady chain of descending notes, you can challenge yourself to a branch-by-branch search to locate the motionless bird, and then challenge yourself again to make sure you haven't mixed it up with the very similar Plaintive Cuckoo (*Cacomantis merulinus*). Long-tailed Parakeets (*Psittacula longicauda*) here compete with Laced Woodpeckers (*Picus vittatus*) and Common Flamebacks (*Dinopium javanense*) for nesting holes. In the middle storey Red Turtle Doves (*Streptopelia tranquebarica*) croon and bubble to each other, while Spotted Doves (*Streptopelia chinensis*) feed on the shaded road.

This is a very good site for the big raptors. Grey-headed Fish-eagles (*Ichthyophaga ichthyaetus*) began nesting here

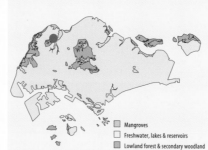

Mangroves
Freshwater, lakes & reservoirs
Lowland forest & secondary woodland

two years ago, as birds spread from the more heavily forested reservoirs of the central catchment, and Changeable Hawk-eagles (*Spizaetus cirrhatus*) have been nesting here for some time. White-bellied Sea-eagles (*Haliaeetus leucogaster*) have been present for many years; they like to use the old radio masts on the adjacent land as nest sites.

From swamp to reservoir

The swamp at the end of the road used to be well known for holding small numbers of Lesser Whistling Ducks (*Dendrocygna javanica*). They disappeared for some years, but now a pair is back. The species seems to have been doing well recently, and like the raptors they may be spreading. Black-backed Swamphens (*Porphyrio indicus*) are a local speciality here, and although they keep over to the far side of the swamp, you can catch a glimpse of a huge red bill or a dark body moving cautiously through the vegetation. The swamphens usually retreat at the sight of the first birdwatcher or fisherman, who may flush a Yellow Bittern (*Ixobrychus sinensis*) or a Cinnamon Bittern (*Ixobrychus cinnamomeus*) from the reeds, or disturb a clucking moorhen.

Butterflies can be good here too. Three of the most diverse groups are the Emigrants and Grass Yellows (family

Opposite, clockwise from top left: *In swampy forest where fresh water trends into the back-mangroves, a Laced Woodpecker* (Picus vittatus) *excavates its nest; the caterpillar of the Autumn Leaf butterfly* (Doleschallia bisaltide) *found in shaded humid vegetation is softly spiny with orange and iridescent blue spots; Blue-tailed Bee-eater* (Merops philippinus) *can hawk for dragonflies over freshwater ponds and reservoirs; the bright red fruit capsule of Simpoh Air* (Dillenia suffruticosa) *with its small red seeds in each compartment is a source of food for birds such as small pigeons and bulbuls along the edge of the water.*

difrom groups are the Emigrants and Grass Yellows (family *Pieridae*) especially because for several of them the *Albizia* trees are the caterpillars' food plant; the Bush Browns and their relatives (Family Nymphalidae) that require grasses for their larvae; and a range of Little Blues (Family Lycaenidae). None of them seems to need the swamp, but they all like the dappled sunlight.

Past the old pumphouse, the view changes again; the swamp was merely a precursor to the wide open reservoir. Across the water, a few Great Egrets (*Casmerodius albus*), can be seen perching in the *Dillenia* shrubs and a Purple Heron (*Ardea purpurea*) stands on the grassy bank. Over the water surface White-winged Terns (*Chlidonias leucopterus*) may be dancing in flight, but a few have settled on the railings at the pumphouse, jostling for position with each other. Because this is such a good place to see a range of wildlife, it will now be jointly managed by government and the local Nature Society. There's no doubt that the reservoir and its swampy margins, artificial though they may be, have increased bird abundance and diversity. A good morning's birdwatching here will yield 50 species or more, across a wide range of woodland, swamp and open water habitats.

Above: *Freshwater birds such as the Yellow Bittern* (Ixobrychus sinensis) *are common but they seldom emerge from the dense pond vegetation.*

Above: *Kranji Reservoir, with small, artificial floating islands, thickly planted with water-loving vegetation, separates Neo Tiew Lane from the more industrial parts of Singapore.*

Freshwater Change

Singapore has 7,000 km (4,350 miles) of drains, and 32 canalized rivers. This is equivalent to 10 km (6 miles) of drain per square kilometre (0.4 sq miles) of land. Brackish drains leading from the sea contain a range of fish species that can tolerate low levels of salinity, including *Scatophaga argus*, a marine species that can intrude upstream, and introduced freshwater Mozambique Tilapia (*Oreochromis mossambicus*) that can intrude downstream. Freshwater drains include an array of frogs, introduced guppies, the Mosquito-fish *Gambusia affinis*, as well as Tilapia that attract feeding egrets, herons and Monitor Lizards.

Only a few natural forest streams now exist in Singapore, and they are important because they are the home of several freshwater crabs endemic to the main island. Because they are not found anywhere else in the world, Singapore has a special responsibility to ensure their well-being. Fortunately all three occur within the nature reserves, though their tiny populations make them inherently vulnerable. Furthermore, all three of the endemic crabs have been discovered and named since 1985. The first was Johnson's Freshwater Crab (*Irmengardia johnsoni*) (1985) found in both the central nature reserves; next was the Singapore Freshwater Crab (*Johora singaporensis*) (1986) from Bukit Timah Nature Reserve and two small streams further to the west. Last was the Swamp Forest Crab (*Parathelphusa reticulata*) (1990) found only in Nee Soon. These crabs are small, inconspicuous and possibly susceptible to changes in climate and acidity that will be outside Singapore's control.

Above: *The American Bullfrog* (Rana catesbiana) *is imported for food, and sometimes escapes into freshwater habitats, but seldom survives long in the unsuitable tropical conditions and is not known to breed successfully – yet!*

Lakes and reservoirs

Singapore's 17 reservoirs now form the bulk of all freshwater ecosystems. Natural lakes are rare in South-East Asia, and all lakes in Singapore are artificial. The reservoirs, created from 1867 onwards, therefore contain a strange mix of adaptable native and introduced species. The reservoirs were created in the sequence shown in the table below.

In spite of being artificial, the reservoirs are now of considerable interest, especially those with forested surroundings. These provide suitable habitat for breeding colonies of herons – for example in Kranji – and for nest sites of the Grey-headed Fish-eagle adjacent to the waterline. Singapore is one of the best localities in Asia to see this bird, and there is little doubt that the populations of big introduced fishes, such as carp and tilapia, support a much higher population density of this eagle, as well as White-bellied Sea-eagles, than could be supported by native fish species.

Between them, various birds have set up a local fish market where everyone gets a fair share. Eagles and Ospreys pluck the giant carp from the surface when the fish come up to gulp air. Grey Herons (*Ardea cinerea*) will nest near fresh water but they more often feed along the coast, whereas the Purple Herons hunt alone for freshwater eels and frogs. Great Egrets have a stand-and-wait technique (though they have also been seen taking fish from the surface with a clumsy helicopter method), whereas Little Egrets (*Egretta garzetta*) stir up the mud with one foot and chase after little fishes and invertebrates they have disturbed.

Kingfishers also specialize: Collared Kingfishers are mainly coastal or birds of secondary woodland, and White-throated Kingfishers (*Halcyon smyrnensis*) mainly take grasshoppers and other terrestrial insects, though they do dive as well. Migrant Common Kingfishers (*Alcedo atthis*) tend to sit over the edge of open ponds, choosing a well-placed twig from which to keep watch, whereas the resident Blue-eared

Size and age of Singapore's reservoirs		
	Date	Surface area (hectares/acres)
MacRitchie	1867	106 (262)
	(modified 1891–94, 1901–05, 1907)	
Lower Peirce	1907–1910	59 (146)
Upper Seletar	1920–21	350 (865)
	(modified 1939–40, 1967–69)	
Upper Peirce	1972–74	320 (791)
Kranji	1970–75	750 (1,853)
Pandan	1972–74	180 (445)
Tekong	1977–78	74 (183)
Murai	1976–81	200 (494)
Poyan and Tengeh	1976–81	610 (1,507)
Sarimbun	1976–81	75 (185)
Jurong Lake	1983	80 (198)
Lower Seletar	1983–84	360 (890)
Bedok	1981–84	88 (217)
Marina Bay	2005–08	95 (235)
Punggol	2010	33 (82)
Serangoon	2010	45 (111)

Opposite: The transition between the more inland freshwater swamp forest and the more nearly coastal back-mangroves is marked by sogginess of the ground, an abundance of pole-sized trees, and aerial roots poking up from the poorly aerated soil.

Kingfishers (*Alcedo meninting*) prefer forested edges. Both of them take little fish, water beetles and larvae of other insects. A kingfisher that does surprisingly well in Singapore is the Stork-billed Kingfisher (*Pelargopsis capensis*), found from mangroves and tidal creeks to the reservoirs, streams in the freshwater swamp forest and even ponds in the botanic gardens. Its 8-cm (3-in) bill is better adapted to seizing bulkier prey than that of any of the other kingfishers.

The reservoirs variously support between seven and 32 species of freshwater fishes, but many of these are not native. Richest in fish is MacRitchie Reservoir within the Central Catchment Nature Reserve, with 14 of its 29 species being native. MacRitchie scores well because of its shaded banks and connection to several forest streams, though it is easily accessible and therefore vulnerable to having exotic species released there by the well-meaning members of the public. Poorest is Murai Reservoir, with only one of its ten fishes being native. In general it seems that native freshwater fishes are more abundant in those reservoirs created at inland sites, whereas the reservoirs created by damming off tidal estuaries have failed to acquire a native freshwater fish fauna. All, however, acquire introduced species such as carp, catfish and tilapia, either to improve fishing or through propitious acts to improve spiritual merit by releasing animals.

These figures tend to emphasize how unnatural deepwater lakes are in the region. There are few lake-adapted fishes, none of them native to Singapore, and the true freshwater fish fauna is found in the small streams and trickles within the undisturbed forest.

The forested margins of MacRitchie Reservoir also make it good for dragonflies and damselflies, of which 24 species have been recorded recently, and it also scores well for amphibians. Yet it contains not a single freshwater snail, conceivably because of past treatment (now discontinued) with copper sulphate for the control of water quality and algal growth. Surprisingly best for molluscs is Jurong Lake, which is surrounded by public parks and lawns.

Right: Food items from both the water, such as prawns and small fish, and from grassland, such as grasshoppers and crickets, provide a living for the White-throated Kingfisher (Halcyon smyrnensis). In many circumstances it can live independently of fresh water.

Opposite: The reservoirs created progressively over the past century have vastly expanded the amount of open water surface, a scarce habitat type in South-East Asia but one that is suited to a number of fish-eating raptors.

Below: One of the commoner but most decorative damselflies is the Ornate Coraltail (Ceriagrion cerinorubellum); it catches insects such as flies and mosquitoes in flight and can contribute to the control of their populations.

Freshwater swamp forest

Though Singapore has little in the way of freshwater swamp forest, what remains is of disproportionate interest. For one thing, it contains many of the most endangered Singapore flora and fauna at just one site. Secondly, the foundational studies on freshwater swamp forest were done in, or based out of, Singapore by the botanist John Corner from 1929 onwards.

The key difference between peat swamp forest and freshwater swamp forest is that the first is dependent largely on rain, and the second is mainly dependent on flooding through more or less prolonged spill-over from adjacent water bodies. Freshwater swamp forest can contain small amounts of peat, and since every forest site naturally receives rain, the distinctions between the two types are partly a matter of degree, not absolute difference. Corner firmly positioned Singapore's representatives as freshwater swamp forest, not peat swamp,

and was clear that freshwater swamp forest is a developmental precursor of the latter. Only when the building of a significant peat dome has begun, with raised marginal levees that hinder the intrusion of floodwater, and with the centre of the dome standing above its surroundings, can dependence on rainwater be clearly demonstrated.

On this basis, Nee Soon is rightly classified as freshwater swamp forest. It has peat, but no peat dome, and much of the water level is determined by the stream network. Ground penetrating radar is limited in its effectiveness by groundwater conditions, but a single long transect has been surveyed at Nee Soon swamp forest, down to a depth of 2 m (6 ft 6 in). This showed successive but irregular layering of sandy and peaty soils, small-scale shearing points where an area of ground seemed to have subsided and irregular troughs that could indicate old palaeo drainage channels. These small-scale features (tens of centimetres in size) perhaps show where a network of streams in the past

Above: The Water Canna (Canna indica) *is an introduced plant, with small brilliant red flowers and spiky, pale green, water repellent seed capsules, that is gradually spreading in Singapore and working its way into areas of secondary growth along waterways.*

Opposite: Because the Nee Soon freshwater swamp forest is one of Singapore's conservation jewels, with high diversity, endemic species, and very small populations of each one, access has to be restricted; it also has historical importance and is used as a source of plant materials for propagating rare species.

Right: Claoxylon indicum *is a tall shrub or small tree on which the flowers are set in long string-like panicles. It grows abundantly in the secondary vegetation that springs up over damp soils after disturbance, or the abandonment of agriculture.*

had changed course, and subsequently been infilled by the natural processes of soil formation.

Shortly after Corner was appointed to the staff of the Botanic Garden, he found that an extensive tract of such forest was being felled at the western end of Mandai Road to make way for the expansion of the Upper Seletar reservoir. He made some initial studies there, and followed this up in 1932–33 by studying another patch at Jurong (being felled as it was being discovered, to turn it into a pineapple plantation!), and continued his studies at the eastern end of Mandai Road until 1940–41. At the same time he was exploring freshwater swamp forest at Sedili in southeast Johor (1929–41), Pontian (1930–40) and Terengganu (1932–35). Most of this work was not published for another 40 years.

Corner is popularly known for having used trained Pigtailed Macaques (*Macaca nemestrina*) to collect flowers, fruits and leaves from the crowns of forest trees for identification, a relatively small step from their traditional use to collect ripe coconuts in east coast villages. Though it had not been recorded by zoologists in Singapore, Corner himself claimed to see this species wild in Mandai, as well as the now very rare Banded Leaf-monkey (*Presbytis femoralis*).

Though the Jurong and most of the Mandai swamp forests have long gone, they were evidently quite distinct. That at Jurong had only about 200 species of angiosperm plants, that at Mandai at least 320. Both were poor in dipterocarps, with only four or five species, but Mandai had far more euphorbs (25 as against five), legumes (11 versus four) and nutmegs (17 versus five). Both had good representation of ferns, Rubiaceae and Annonaceae, but of this last family out of 21 species in all, only five were shared by both sites. Out of 26 species of figs, only nine were shared. Corner did not collect hydrological or soil data, but his impression was that conditions were similar at all his sites, and that differences reflected the relative influence of phytogeography (the geographic distribution of plants species), Jurong sharing more species with Sumatra and Mandai sharing more species with Borneo and the Malay Peninsula.

Three things came out of this. First was Corner's idea that even within such a small territory as Singapore, even in places just a few kilometres apart, there could be significant phytogeographical differences. This has not been followed up, but herbarium specimens and scraps of remnant vegetation today probably still make it possible to test this idea further. Second was his concept of a Riau Pocket, an ancient basin of swampy forest with its special hydrology and array of characteristic plants that probably occupied the centre of the exposed Sunda Shelf between the Malay Peninsula, Sumatra and Borneo during the Pleistocene at periods of low sea level, such as the period 8,000 years ago. Third was Corner's elaboration of his 'Durian Theory'. This proposed that angiosperms evolved from ancestral stout, pithy-stemmed monocarpic trees with a terminal inflorescence and large spiny dehiscent fruits, the seeds enclosed by waxy arils, towards increasingly slender, many-branched forms with small, smooth, non-dehiscent fruits lacking

Top: The invasive weed Neptunia plena *may not be instantly recognisable as a member of the traditional pea and bean group, now split into several related families, but it is closely related to the better known mimosa.*

Above: Canavalia cathartica *is another member of the pea and bean group, with more recognisable pink flowers.*

Above: The Giant Mahang (Macaranga gigantea) *is a member of the freshwater swamp forest community and also found in other forest types. The leaf is 40cm (15 in) across.*

Left: Coccinea grandis *is a member of the Cucurbitaceae family (cucumbers and allies) pollinated by bees; the name of the genus is based on its red fruits.*

Above: Also found growing near water is the delicate Ludwigia octovalvis, *its foliage covered with fine hairs. This is one of six* Ludwigia *species in Singapore.*

Right: A classic plant of the lower reaches of rivers is the Nipah Palm (Nypa fruticans) *whose different parts have many uses: leaves for thatch and cigarette papers, fruits as food and for alcohol.*

an aril. The theory was based supposedly on a single visit to Nee Soon in 1944 with the Japanese botanist Professor Kwan Koriba during which they found the fruits of the tree *Sloanea javanica*. During the war Japanese policy was to maintain scientific institutions, such as the botanic gardens, and Corner was never interned, giving him tremendous opportunities both for botanical theorizing and for the rescuing of libraries and archives threatened by military action.

History and botanists have hardly noticed the first of Corner's ideas about the swamp forest. They have readily accepted the second idea, the Riau Pocket, but they have been unkind to the Durian Theory, as they have to Corner's overall concepts of plant evolution expressed in his book on *The Life of Plants*. 'Antiquated and unjustified in light of our present state of knowledge', according to Karl Niklas of Cornell University. Never mind; the Durian Theory, even if misguided or wrong, is one of those rare pieces of sweeping evolutionary vision based

on an intimate knowledge of tropical natural history that acts as a stimulus to others and is valid on those terms as a scientific challenge to be built upon.

The earliest record of freshwater swamp forest in Singapore seems to be from a book of watercolour sketches published in Germany in 1876. One sketch, titled 'Path across the swamp (Changi)' clearly shows the typical blackwater conditions and an array of swamp forest plants such as Sealingwax Palm (*Cyrtostachys renda*), Nipah Palm (*Nypa fruticans*), Screwpine (*Pandanus* sp.), as well as a very realistic Mahang (*Macaranga gigantea*). Now there are only some 50 ha (124 acres) of freshwater swamp forest at the main site at Nee Soon, with a couple of other scraps at the very edges of the Upper Seletar reservoir. With small patches remaining behind the mangroves in very secluded spots, and old regenerating swamp with a tiny fragment of the original in the western military area, the total for Singapore is less than 60 ha (148 acres) altogether. Because of this and the concentration of many rare

Above: The water in freshwater swamp forest is somewhat acidic, contains tannins from decaying leaf litter as well as a fair sediment load, and is lit by sunflecks penetrating the canopy; within the submerged leaf litter are various small fish, caddis and dragonfly larvae, crabs and prawns.

Opposite: In disturbed areas an array of small and pretty wetland plants forms a delicate tangle just above the water surface; they include the yellow Neptunia *and candy pink* Merremia hederacea.

species at a single location, Nee Soon is now the prime conservation locality in Singapore.

Up in the trees live the Banded Leaf-monkeys. Once apparently fairly widespread within Singapore, they were thought to have disappeared by the 1960s. Later a few, estimated at a dozen, were found to be still living in Nee Soon in the freshwater swamp forest. Accidents happened; the last female within Bukit Timah Nature Reserve was killed by dogs in 1986. But the estimates gradually crept up, to 20 or 30, and most recently to perhaps 50 or 60 individuals living in half a dozen troops, all within this small area. If any animal deserves an identity crisis, it is this one. It was first given the name *Presbytis femoralis* by William Martin in 1838, based on a specimen from Singapore. In 1940 F. N. Chasen of the Raffles Museum, taking a more comprehensive view of the geographical variation shown by mammal populations across South-East Asia, made it merely one local representative of a much more widespread species, *Presbytis melalophos*, extending from Sumatra to Thailand and western Borneo, and this is how it made its way into the standard mammal textbooks. In the 1970s work on vocalizations and behaviour began to question such variation again and, only in the past four or five years, work on DNA has shown that *P. femoralis* is indeed a valid species, confined to Singapore and adjacent parts of Johor.

With this reappraisal, the Singapore population, tiny as it is and only gradually increasing over the past few decades, is seen as a much higher conservation priority. Singapore is its type locality, the locality from which it was first named, and thus important for all future reference. Even with as few as 60 individuals, the Singapore population suddenly becomes a significant component of a species that is only found to its northern limit perhaps 100 km (62 miles) to the north, a limit that has still not been pinpointed. The identity of leaf-monkeys in Endau-Rompin and in the freshwater swamp forests of eastern Johor and eastern Pahang needs to be reassessed.

Why they are confined to freshwater swamp forest in Nee Soon is not known. Their apparently

Opposite: One of the few species of wild orchids to have survived in Singapore is Cymbidium finlaysonianum, *whose honey-coloured blossoms are arranged in a long hanging spray, taking advantage of the plant's position growing on a vertical soil bank. Many varieties of this orchid have been brought into cultivation.*

Right: Tree snails in the genus Amphidromus *are unusual in having a left-handed spiral to the shell, but Singapore's population of the Green Tree Snail* (Amphidromus atricallosus), *found mostly in freshwater swamp forest, is still more unusual amongst the unusual, in having reverted to the normal right-handed spiral found in other snails.*

closest relatives in Peninsular Malaysia are fairly widespread in tall forest from the extreme lowlands to the mountain slopes. Possibly Nee Soon was the last place from which they were not hunted out, and their extreme shyness may be a result of past hunting from which they have still to recover. Past records from other parts of Singapore suggest that if their numbers can be increased, they will gradually be able to spread to other forest habitats. The first in-depth study of them only began in 2008 and there is still much to learn, but so far there is no specific known characteristic of the swamp forest that makes them dependent on this forest type alone.

In the streams are the swamp forest crab, Johnson's Freshwater Crab, and the Torrent Prawn (*Macrobrachium brachyteles*). On land the Green Tree Snail (*Amphidromus atricallosus*) occurs in the swamp forest at Nee Soon and on Pulau Tekong and the local population has been described as an endemic subspecies (*A. a. temasek*) as recently as 2010, though its presence has long been known. Climbers include

rare species of lipstick flowers (*Aeschynanthus* spp.). The ground flora includes orchids that are locally rare and endangered such as *Diaenia ophrydis*. Plants known only from here include the Climbing Moss (*Papillidiopsis bruchii*), the orchid *Bulbophyllum macranthum* and the White-flowered Kopsia (*Kopsia singapurensis*). Though most are widely distributed outside Singapore, their concentration in Nee Soon makes it a vital area for conservation at national level.

Among the animals, the Blue-spotted Bush-frog (*Rhacophorus cyanopunctatus*) is a Nee Soon speciality, together with quite a few small freshwater fish. So is the dragonfly *Tetrathema irregularis*. These are all small creatures and, with the possible but unlikely exception of the monkeys, no large animals are known to require freshwater swamp forest to the exclusion of other habitat types.

Aphids are not the most common nor the most conspicuous of plant pests in South-East Asia, where scale insects, plant hoppers, bagworms and leaf miners gain more attention. But they are interesting. One predominantly Asian genus is *Anomalosiphon*, with only six species, most closely related to an Australian genus and after that to a genus in Brazil and Peru. *Anomalosiphon murphyi* was described in 1994 from specimens collected in Nee Soon swamp forest. They had had to wait more than 20 years in a museum cabinet before they were named, having been collected in January 1973. The species is only known from females that bear live young and are perhaps parthenogenetic (able to reproduce asexually), feeding on the sap of understorey trees including *Rourea* and *Xanthophyllum*. They have also been collected at Bukit Timah, in the same month, and at Gunung Mulu National Park in Sarawak four years later: these are true forest-living aphids. No photograph is known to exist.

Many of the plants and animals in the freshwater swamp forest are only indirectly dependent on the water. But there are whole groups that are strictly water dependent. In particular, several groups of insects require fresh water in which to deposit their eggs, with fully aquatic larvae. In the whole of Peninsular Malaysia there are 236 species of dragonflies and damselflies, 38 per cent of them being the slender-bodied, more forest stream-dependent damselflies. Given the huge changes in vegetation of Singapore since 1819, it is remarkable that 126 species have been recorded locally. You might predict that the delicate damselflies would have suffered disproportionately from forest clearance and the loss of natural streams, yet they still make up 33 per cent of Singapore's total. Somehow the remaining streams in the nature reserves, the forested edges of the reservoirs and shaded patches of swamp elsewhere must be adequate to maintain their populations. Another factor is mobility; the steady trickle of new dragonfly records suggests that individuals of at least the bigger, stronger fliers must be wandering over from Peninsular Malaysia.

Dragonfly mobility is also demonstrated by the records from a pond newly created by the National Parks Board in an area of open turf at Labrador Nature

Reserve. Within 24 months of the pond's creation, 34 dragonfly species had been recorded there, more than a quarter of Singapore's total. This just exceeded the totals of 33 each found in long-established parks such as Bishan and Toa Payoh Town Park, which are among Singapore's top dragonfly spots, and well above that for any single reservoir though still below the total for the Central Catchment Nature Reserve as a whole. Evidently, if habitat is made available, many dragonflies will find it.

Above: An invasive species of reservoirs, ponds and slow-flowing rivers, the Golden Apple Snail (Pomacea canaliculata) has been introduced accidentally into many tropical countries and gives away its presence by laying masses of pink eggs; so far it has not invaded forested streams.

Left: The Scarlet Grenadier (Lathrecista asiatica) *is one of the commoner dragonflies in Singapore, with the caveat that it prefers forest habitats, where it flies fast through dappled sun and shade before settling briefly on the tips of twigs.*

Below: The diversity of dragonflies is still poorly understood, and even urban parks such as that at Toa Payoh can support a quarter of all Singapore's species. The diversity of plant structure with floating and emergent leaves certainly helps.

7
City Living

Wildlife in Singapore finds a place to live around and even upon the many buildings characteristic of a densely populated city. Besides the network of nature reserves, parks, park connectors and roadside trees, Singapore has programmes to develop vertical, skyrise and rooftop greenery. All of these help to extend and elaborate the environment available to a range of plants and small animals compatible with people, and satisfy the need to keep in touch with nature through recreation, education and relaxation.

Left: Roadside trees and neighbourhood parks provide substantial greenery between skyscrapers even within high density parts of the city.

Jurong Central Park: green space in an industrial centre

A public park placed as this one is, between dense housing on one side and factories and light industry on the other, has to cater to heavy use. It was first designed with an unusual thematic layout, with sections of garden designed as board games: such as snakes and ladders, and ludo. Paths and seats are arranged around these densely planted centres of activity, while the grass lawns are much used on public holidays by workers from the local factories. Picnicking is the norm.

It's no surprise that the birds enjoy the benefits of the picnics too. Feral Pigeons (*Columba livia*) are common here; they nest in crevices in the MRT (Mass Rapid Transit) overhead railway lines, under the station roof and under the air conditioning units on the outside walls of the apartments that overshadow the park. Brahminy Kites (*Haliastur indus*) circle in the sky, Collared Kingfishers make their calls, Sunda Pygmy Woodpeckers (*Dendrocopos moluccensis*) peck on trees, White-breasted Waterhens (*Amaurornis phoenicurus*) dart around and even Javan Mynas (*Acridotheres javanicus*) shower in the wetland. All these birds have been sighted in the park, to name just a few.

The park has now been opened for ten years; before that it was an industrial site, so the ornamental trees are still maturing. A shallow wetland has been created towards one side of the park, one of the less frequented areas which is full of dragonflies and frogs. Recently, Jurong Central Park has been refreshed with new designs and new plantings. The Gelam Trees (*Melaleuca cajuputi*) are doing well; they have been planted close to the wetland so their roots are in soggy ground, not unlike their natural habitat in shallow coastal swamps behind sand dunes. If you crush a leaf in your fingers you can smell the very aromatic cajuputi oil. It's a corruption of the Malay name *kayu putih*, white wood. They're easily recognizable by the aroma, and also by the shredding bark – it is a distinctive tree that lent its name to Kampung Gelam down near the city.

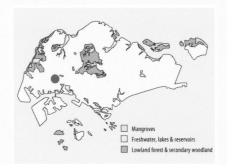

☐ Mangroves
☐ Freshwater, lakes & reservoirs
☐ Lowland forest & secondary woodland

The closest residential blocks are about 100 m (330 ft) away, across the road and the MRT line, with space for trees between the blocks and on the central divider in the two-lane dual carriageway. From the overhead bridge linking the park to the neighbourhood, you are on the same level as the crowns of the African Mahogany (*Khaya grandifolia*) planted in niches between the pedestrian walks, and well above the tops of the South American Tabebuias (*Tabebuia pallida, T. rosea*), the Australian Foxtail Palms (*Wodyetia bifurcata*) and the Hibiscus (*Hibiscus rosa-sinensis*) and Ixora (*Ixora javanica*) hedges skirting the square cut lawns. At times like this the residents may enjoy a cool fresh breeze by opening windows and doors, but on still days it can be muggy and uncomfortable.

Wake-up calls

Long before dawn the Asian Koels (*Eudynamys scolopacea*) start calling, a rising series of ecstatic shouts, echoing off the faces of the buildings. They only arrived in Singapore as a breeding species in the mid-1980s. It was the opening of land throughout the region and the presence of House Crows (*Corvus splendens*) that did it – they found opportunities to parasitize the nests of the crows, orioles and mynas. The crows' numbers have been managed and their population

*Opposite, clockwise from top left: Planting of flowers, shrubs, palms, and small and large trees creates a structurally diverse park with many activity spaces screened from one another; Water Canna (*Canna indica*) and Cat-tail Bulrushes (*Typha angustifolia*) provide many landing platforms and lookout points for insects; a native population of wild Lesser Whistling Ducks (*Dendrocygna javanica*) can be found on lakes within some of the city parks and gardens; steadily maturing trees lead to an increase in aspects of parkland habitat quality such as shade, temperature amelioration, structural complexity, food and potential nest sites.*

Above: *The Common Myna* (Acridotheres tristis) *is facing competition from related mynas introduced more recently, and is common no longer.*

Above: *Another species declining because of introduced competitors is the Green Crested Lizard* (Bronchocela cristatella), *still found in small numbers along hedgerows and in wilder areas.*

has declined, but the mynas seem ever more abundant.

People complain about the noise of the koels; it wakes them too early in the morning, though you might agree that it's one of the most glorious sounds of the city. If you watch a pair long enough, you will see the male craftily lure the crows into chasing him, so that they leave their nest unguarded and the female can sneak quickly in to lay her egg. A distinctive bubbling call is also made by a koel. They make four or five different sounds and nobody has yet worked out exactly what they all mean. The often-heard fluting whistle, on the other hand, is a Black-naped Oriole (*Oriolus chinensis*). It is wonderful to see the flash of brilliant yellow as two or three of them pursue each other through the foliage below.

Sharing the living space

Some of the apartment owners have potted plants on their balconies, cacti, orchids, hibiscus and Japanese bamboo. One balcony has a nesting pair of Olive-backed Sunbirds (*Cinnyris jugularis*). They are bringing material from the park, flying over the dual carriageway, chirping incessantly as they fly back and forth. The purse-shaped nest hangs from a hibiscus twig. It is made of spiders' web and silk (maybe from the seeds of one of the trees in the park), all mixed in with dead leaves and other fragments. It's not very neat but it's too small to be intrusive. The little roof the birds

construct over the nest entrance where the female perches will keep the babies dry in all but the wildest weather; up there on the seventh storey the wind can be strong and the nest swings wildly from time to time, but the birds don't seem to mind.

As the evening draws in, curtains are drawn and lights go on. The park below quietens in the dusk as people leave, perhaps to search out some dinner in the nearest food court. House Geckos (*Hemidactylus frenatus*) click and chuckle as they scamper to join a companion behind the awning of a shop. Geckos are really cute. They can't be kept out of open-fronted buildings, and any stallholder who wants to maintain his 'A' certificate for food hygiene will have a running battle with geckos. Above the sounds of cooking pans from one of the restaurants, an occasional myna is still calling, late on its way to join the communal roost down by the junction with the traffic lights – for some reason they always seem to choose the noisiest, most brightly lit places – and suddenly there is a tremendous racket as a screaming flock of Rainbow Lorikeets (*Trichoglossus haematodus*), escaped from somewhere and now breeding in tree-holes, come rocketing along the space between the residential blocks.

Down at ground level a House-shrew (*Suncus murinus*), a Chinese 'money-mouse', makes a tinkling sound like the dropping of coins as she emerges cautiously into the darkness to follow her usual route. She is protected by her strong musky scent: no fastidious cat will touch her tonight.

Density, density!

Singapore's more than five million people live within less than 40 per cent of the land area. Greenery of all descriptions covers 46 per cent, roads cover 12 per cent, and then there are industrial areas, business districts, airports and other hard surfaces to be considered. So that although the average population density for the nation is 7,126 people per sq km (0.4 sq miles), the density within residential areas may be in the order of 17,800 people per sq km. The reasons for Singapore's high-rise approach to life are obvious.

In 2010 there were 597,746 private and other cars (excluding taxis) on the road. With public and commercial vehicles as well, they could take up around one tenth of the available road surface, if they were all in use at the same time – which of course they are not. Roads occupy about 85 sq km (33 sq miles), which is about equal to the 33 sq km (13 sq miles) in the four Nature Reserves, the 23 sq km (9 sq miles) in parks, open spaces, park connectors and playgrounds and 26 sq km (10 sq miles) of roadside greenery.

How can nature possibly be compatible with such pressures? One answer is that much wildlife is itself living in the fast track. Even the MRT lines – the Mass Rapid Transit railways – support bird life. At one surface station (naturally there are no birds in the underground stations) either on the platform, the rails or the concrete parapet, there have been Javan Mynas, Common Mynas, Feral Pigeons, Spotted Doves, two species of kingfishers, a Cattle Egret (*Bubulcus ibis*), Little Egrets, Eurasian Tree-sparrows (*Passer montanus*), Yellow-vented Bulbuls (*Pycnonotus goiavier*), Olive-backed Sunbirds, Asian Glossy Starlings (*Aplonis panayensis*) and House Crows.

Because nothing grows on the tracks, and trees are not allowed to overhang the line, there is virtually no food available for them so most birds merely pass through. But the concrete supports do provide nesting places, in between the longitudinal sections for Feral Pigeons and in drainage holes for the mynas and sparrows.

Above: *The Yellow-vented Bulbul* (Pycnonotus goiavier) *is one of the city's commonest birds, usually seen in pairs. Their lilting song is a familiar sound.*

Below: *The tiny Olive-backed Sunbird* (Cinnyris jugularis) *is able to make a living from the nectar and pollen of many roadside shrubs and flowers.*

Green buildings

Many buildings in the central business district now have some sort of green rooftop, or vertical greenery on outside walls or substantial greenery in outdoor planting boxes. Of course this requires measures to ensure proper load bearing and drainage. The benefits for beautification, temperature control and energy consumption can be substantial, though no studies have yet been undertaken to determine their influence on rooftop wildlife. Certainly a range of small birds makes use of them.

On older buildings, plant life may arrive of its own accord. It is not uncommon to see a small fig such as *Ficus religiosa* taking root at the junction between wall and drainpipe, or a cluster of ferns along the edge of a roof. But these occur at places not designed for them, and figs certainly need to be removed before their roots begin to cause physical damage. Caring for buildings as well as nature demands a strong commitment to upkeep and maintenance.

Above: Planting boxes with dense creepers trailing downwards can substantially reduce temperatures inside buildings, leading to energy savings through reduced air conditioning and smaller utility bills for the building owners. They help buildings such as this city-centre university hall to blend in with the adjacent park, and also reduce temperatures at street level for pedestrians.

Left: Rooftop greenery comprising mainly small Cinnamon trees (Cinnamomum iners) *planted above a multi-storey carpark greatly reduces the unsightliness of concrete and provides green layering that adds to the three-dimensional effect created by the roadside trees, here Rain Trees* (Albizia saman).

Opposite: Hardly recognisable as a scene along Singapore's busiest shopping district, Orchard Road, planted orange heliconias and foliage shrubs are mixed with small trees such as cinnamon. The result is a shady walkway with dappled light, and a green environment for people and nature.

Commuting

Every year, wildlife in the city is boosted by migrant birds arriving from countries such as Japan, China, Vietnam and Thailand. Some, like migrant Peregrine Falcons (*Falco peregrinus*), gravitate towards the faces of tall buildings that resemble the natural cliffs they are familiar with. None breeds locally, but for several weeks or months a single bird or a pair may frequent a particular window ledge or parapet, which is a handy base from which to chase a passing pigeon. Other birds will remain in roadside trees and parks, or move through the city along green corridors. Even Oriental Honey-buzzards (*Pernis ptilorynchus*) can be seen in places like Tanglin and Somerset Road that are well within the city itself, close to the shopping hub.

Local residents also commute daily, but over shorter distances. Crows, mynas, glossy starlings and bulbuls all form communal roosts where they congregate around dusk. Mynas typically prefer places that are noisy and brightly lit at night, such as busy road junctions. Crows need tall trees, though their numbers have gone down over the past couple of decades and their communal roosts are less striking than they used to be. Glossy starlings often mix with mynas, or roost in groups on high tension wires, while Yellow-vented Bulbuls choose thick vegetation or reed beds. In each case, individual birds or pairs, or small groups, will fan out early the following morning for the day's foraging. Green spaces in the city are therefore not self-contained and sustainable units, but depend on animals networking between them; mobile pigeons, bulbuls and orioles will carry seeds from one park to another.

Above: At least three species of plants including the Bodhi Fig (Ficus religiosa) can be seen growing on the parapets of an old city building; the fig will need to be removed before its roots cause substantial damage by cracking plasterwork and the underlying bricks.

Condominium living

Singaporeans share their homes with a variety of smaller wildlife, some of it welcome and some of it not. Birds nesting on the balcony are all very well, and interesting to watch through the window, but nobody likes cockroaches, household ants in the sugar or potter wasps entering the open window and making a mess of the curtains or blinds by building their clay nests in the folds. Silverfish damage books by eating the glue in the bindings, dust mites live in the mattress and pillow and can worsen asthma or allergies, and weevils may live in the rice.

If you don't dispose of rubbish promptly, tiny red-eyed fruit flies can be irritating in the kitchen, but they do no harm. House flies are more of a nuisance as they can bring in contaminants, and every Singaporean is aware of the risks posed by mosquitoes as vectors of dengue fever and malaria. In damp bathrooms, you may find little spindle-shaped grey-brown cases of the Wall Bagworm Moth

Above: The Javan or White-vented Myna (Acridotheres javanicus) *has been introduced to many tropical countries, partly through the captive bird trade.*

Below: From the temperate zone to the tropics, the Little Tern (Sterna albifrons) *nests on bare sandy ground, where the eggs and chicks may be vulnerable to accidental disturbance.*

(*Phereoeca uterella*); each contains the larva, not the adult which is seldom recognized. They make their bags out of tough silk and fragments of grit and dust, and gradually creep up the wall feeding on fungus or other organic matter on its surface. Also seen on the bathroom wall are tiny toilet moth-flies (Family Psychodidae), only two or three millimetres across the wings. Most of these creatures (except for the mosquitoes) pose relatively low risk and all are easily controlled by straightforward and simple household cleanliness and hygiene. It is difficult and unnecessary to eliminate them completely.

Attitudes are a little more ambivalent towards geckos and jumping spiders. Some people cannot abide geckos and resort to horrific control measures with a rolled-up newspaper or, worse, a can of insect spray. Others consider geckos to be rather cheerful creatures, or even lucky, while some maintain the middle ground that geckos don't do much harm and are useful in controlling flies, mosquitoes and moths. Jumping spiders have a special place in Singapore

culture. The Fighting Spider (*Thiania bhamoensis*) caught by schoolboys and kept in a matchbox to pit in contests against those of friends is an outdoor dweller, usually found on the leaves of plants, but the indoor species such as the tweed-coloured Housefly Catcher (*Plexippus paykulli*) are definitely useful in controlling insects within the house.

Breakfast on the go

After 12 hours of rest during the night, every animal needs to find food as soon as possible upon waking. The mynas may head straight to the food court where they can find scraps at tables, but nectar-feeding birds will head for the flowers for a quick shot of energy-giving sugars. The sunbirds may be attracted by Canna Lilies (*Canna generalis*), or gingers or ixoras, but they will find that not all the ixoras are worthwhile; there are distinct nectar-yielding and non-nectar varieties.

Right: The layering of vegetation can be achieved by planting at different levels on buildings, by planting species that grow to differing heights, and by planting trees that are themselves layered, such as the pagoda growth form of the introduced Dwarf Geometry Tree (in the foreground) or Spiny Black Olive (Bucida molineti) originally from the Bahamas.

Opposite: Various aquatic plants are grown in ponds and slow-flowing water bodies in order to remove excessive nutrients from the water; one of them is the native Cat-tail or Lesser Bulrush (Typha angustifolia), a very widespread species in the tropical, subtropical and even temperate zones.

see a butterfly or two, especially along turnings just off the main traffic route.

Some 'shops' run 24-hour business; others have definite opening hours. The Yellow Turnera (*Turnera ulmifolia*) and White Alder (*T. subulata*) are two of the flowers with a very precise daily cycle: perfect for breakfast for bees. Each of these plants has several cultivated varieties, and close observation shows that they have slightly differing flower opening times, one at 07:20 in the morning, another perhaps 15 minutes later.

Left: *The Great Eggfly* (Hypolimnas bolina) *is represented in Singapore by two subspecies and up to four different colour morphs in females, making for great natural variability in this common butterfly.*

Below: *An abundant butterfly of grassland and open places, even in the city centre, is the low-flying Blue Pansy* (Junonia orithya)*, named for the velvety blue-black patches on its upper surface.*

The Yellow-vented Bulbuls, fresh from their roost among the Cat-tail Bulrushes (*Typha angustifolia*) where the surrounding water kept them safe overnight, should be seeking out small sugar-rich fruits. The berries of *Cordia cylindristachys* used to be their favourite first thing in the morning, but this is no longer such a common hedge-plant as it used to be, and instead the bulbuls may be satisfied with the so-called Malayan Cherries (*Muntingia calabura*), or Straits Rhododendron (*Melastoma malabathricum*), or figs.

Butterflies perhaps do not face quite the same urgency. They will typically rest up until the day warms, then go off in search of flowers. In a bid to bring more of them into the city, The Nature Society (Singapore) has been working with property owners and government agencies to plant many more blossoms and food plants along Orchard Road, the prime shopping district in the city centre. It seems to be working. Certainly the side plantings are far richer and more varied than they were and it is not rare to

Things that go bump in the night

At the other end of the day are creatures that need darkness. The commonest bats in the city are the House Bat (*Scotophilus kuhlii*), a plush-furred, rather agile bat, and Lesser Dog-faced Fruit-bats (*Cynopterus brachyotis*). One is an insectivore, feeding on the concentrations of flying termites and other insects around street lights; the other is a frugivore, often roosting under house eaves during the day and emerging to squabble noisily over hard green fruits – especially the fruits of *Palaquium* – during the night.

Even in small scraps of dense vegetation, a park corner or a cluster of greenery in a niche next to a condominium block, you may hear a Collared Scops-owl (*Otus bakkamoena*). It gives a single hoot, repeated at very regular intervals of ten seconds or so. They can keep this up for hours, presumably to maintain contact with each other, and perhaps trying to frighten prey into moving too hastily. But their target is mainly beetles, geckos and other small creatures, not often rodents that would be scared into running away.

Spotted Wood-owls (*Strix seloputo*) are around too, and steadily increasing in number after their arrival in the mid-1980s. These really are rodent eaters, hefty predators with a powerful booming call that might well frighten a passer-by, let alone a small mammal. They have not yet penetrated quite into the city centre, but they are all around it, from Tanglin and the Botanic Gardens to Sentosa Island. In the real city, under the concrete beams of Benjamin Sheares Bridge, you might still be lucky enough to find a Barn Owl (*Tyto alba*).

Parks and roadside trees must be providing enough insect food to support a healthy population of Large-tailed Nightjars (*Caprimulgus macrurus*), because their characteristic calls are very common. Their knock-on-wood call, endlessly repeated, makes a tremendous contrast to the rising shrieks of the koels as they sense the coming dawn. Even the noise of the morning rush hour cannot drown out the sound.

Right: It is debatable whether the Changeable Lizard (Calotes versicolor) arrived in Singapore in the 1980s under its own steam or brought by man, as it has been spreading down the Malay Peninsula for decades.

Invasion of the body snatchers

The daily dramas of life and death can take place on a very small scale. Some wasps are capable of parasitizing caterpillars and spiders, the mother wasp catching one as prey, concealing it in a nice secure spot such as a hole in rotten timber, or in the soil, and laying her eggs in it. We may hope that the victim is not aware of being eaten alive, from the inside out, by the hatchling wasp larvae.

Robber flies have a more direct approach, grabbing a victim when perched or in flight and executing a summary death sentence in order to enjoy the meal.

Singapore used to be home to the Orchid Mantis (*Hymenopus coronatus*), a species of praying mantis coloured white and pink like an orchid flower. It used this camouflage to spring out and catch a flower-visiting insect. Orchid Mantises have not been seen locally for some years, and are probably gone, but there are various spiders that match flower colours and use a similar technique.

Above: Oriental Magpie-robins (Copsychus saularis) *went through a population bottleneck in the 1980s but controls on poaching for the bird trade have enabled them to make a comeback; empty biscuit tins provided as nest sites have also helped at selected places.*

Opposite above: Fruits of various tree species are dispersed by Lesser Dog-faced Fruit-bats (Cynopterus brachyotis), *a species that roosts in small clusters beneath the eaves of less disturbed buildings, whether old or new. Each cluster may house one or two males and a harem of females with their young.*

Opposite below: Though difficult to protect from the exotic food trade, the Malayan Pangolin (Manis javanica) *is still fairly common and can occasionally blunder into gardens or cross busy streets in its nightly search for ant and termite nests. Toothless, it catches them with its long and sticky tongue.*

Close encounters of the furred kind

Various mammals have either learnt how to live with humans or else blissfully ignore them. Siglap, in the southeastern part of Singapore, has a population of Common Palm Civets (*Paradoxurus hermaphroditus*) living in gardens and nearby wooded areas. They are mainly nocturnal, but sometimes emerge in the day as well, and can be seen trotting delicately along a fence, or curled up on the branch of a fruit tree. Some residents find them disconcerting, but they are not likely to confront people directly. Theft of a mango, or a bit of noise and mess inside the roof-space of a house are more likely causes for irritation.

Pangolins (*Manis javanica*) also enter residential areas from time to time, and are sometimes killed on the roads. There is no particular reason for them to come into human habitations, and they are probably just disorientated. Since their food is ants and termites, houses and gardens are unlikely to support them, and like the civets, individuals that are found by people are usually sent back to the nature reserves.

Residents of a big city are often not used to encountering wildlife and may react in very different ways. The taxi driver who finds a pangolin might fondly let it go in the bushes, the householder who sees a Long-tailed Macaque in the garden might feel threatened 'because it was looking at me'. The risks from wildlife cannot be shrugged off: Singapore suffered a number of deaths from Sudden Acute Respiratory Syndrome (SARS) in 2003 – SARS is caused by a virus that is resident in mammals and birds – and avian influenza is another valid but very tiny cause for concern. The risks are extremely small, and generally it is quite sufficient to keep one's distance and just let wild animals go about their normal lives, side by side in the city.

Tough Turf

Land eventually meant for housing or other construction is sometimes prepared years in advance. It is typical to lay red earth, perhaps removed from some other construction or excavation site, directly over the existing surface and build it up to the required height, levelling it and compacting it for future use. This creates an impermeable red clay pan, and if the site is not turfed or built on immediately, it will develop into *Acacia* or *Adinandra* stands or, if wet, into shallow vegetated ponds.

Being shallow, transient puddles after rain can become hot, so the plants are tough. Three or four different types of sedges occur here, together with the Clubmoss (*Lycopodiella cernuum*), a primitive plant halfway between a moss and a fern that can grow surprisingly luxuriant in these conditions. Above the surface of the water is a spangle of yellow blossoms from bladderworts (*Utricularia* spp.) with their special underwater roots bearing little bladder-like insect traps to suck in and digest unwary invertebrates. The big secondary shrub known as Simpoh Air (*Dillenia suffruticosa*) may grow part in and part out of the water. Its large yellow flowers attract bees, and Yellow-vented Bulbuls come for the seeds exposed by the star-shaped pink and white fruits. Common species of frogs can be found in the water, but some of the water birds are more interesting: Red-wattled Lapwings (*Vanellus indicus*) fluting mournfully as they are disturbed, and Common Snipe (*Gallinago gallinago*) and Pintail Snipe (*Gallinago stenura*). White-breasted Waterhens (*Amaurornis phoenicurus*) and Slaty-breasted Rails (*Gallirallus striatus*) may be seen cautiously edging through the vegetation, looking for small pond life to share with their fluffy black chicks. On drier ground,

in sandy spots, the hemiparasitic mauve flower *Burmannia coelestis* sometimes grows, looking a little like an orchid, while the true orchid *Liparis ferruginea* can be found in isolated tufts standing in the water.

But most prepared sites will not be allowed to reach this interesting state. Cow grass will be planted to prevent the site becoming eroded, in readiness for future building, or better quality grasses in areas for other uses. Singapore's 20 golf courses use a range of different turf species such as *Zoysia matrella* and *Cynodon dactylon* for high quality fairways and putting greens. High maintenance, frequent mowing and standardized grass height make a less interesting space for wildlife, but even here things can be found. Javan Mynas will certainly use the fairways for foraging, inserting their bills into crevices in the soil to look for worms and other invertebrates. Paddyfield Pipits (*Anthus rufulus*) scattered singly will take little forward runs then pause to look about. Cattle Egrets, wild migrants anywhere, or perhaps free-flying birds from the zoo or bird park in the western part of

Above: The migrant Barn Swallow (Hirundo rustica) *that arrives in huge numbers each year from continental Asia, is told from resident swallows by a black band separating the rufous throat from its clean-looking white underparts, and long tail streamers.*

Right: Even along concrete-lined drains in the city, the Little Egret (Egretta garzetta) *can make a living feeding on small fish; its yellow toes make it straightforward to tell apart from other species of egrets.*

Opposite: One of the commonest plants in unmanaged second-growth vegetation, the lush and glossy leaves of Simpoh Air (Dillenia suffruticosa) *are as attractive as its perpetually borne yellow blossoms, but its scrambling shape can make it look rather untidy.*

Singapore, will stalk about looking for grasshoppers. The range of species is not very great, but this is a substantial part of the Singapore landscape.

It was in habitat such as this, in the 1960s, that biologists in Singapore contributed to work on the timing of birds' reproductive cycles. In one of the least seasonal climates in the world, where food seemed to be abundant throughout the year, how did birds and other animals time their breeding so precisely each year? It cannot be that surplus food is available when migrants leave, allowing residents to consume more, for the resident species such as Yellow-vented Bulbuls begin breeding while the migrants are still around. Regular sampling showed that defoliating caterpillars increase during the northeast monsoon (December–February) and nocturnal flying insects during January–June. Yellow-vented Bulbuls in Singapore reach their highest muscle weights in February–March, and lowest in June–August. The production of sperm and ova begins in January, with most breeding from then until March followed by a decline in body weight as tissue resources are diverted to moult and the growth of new feathers.

Furthermore, it has been found that bulbuls achieving less than average body weights breed later or not at all in any given year, with females recovering their body weight more efficiently than males. Females in this case probably play a more important role in determining the timing of breeding that can vary by several weeks from year to year.

The study of bird breeding cycles is still grossly inadequate. There is little information published on the timing of reproduction by Javan Mynas, in spite of their being one of Singapore's commonest (but introduced) birds. Hence we are in a poor position to establish any effects of climate change on either the timing or the success of breeding. We do not know how representative bulbuls are of other birds; we do not know if there are fundamental differences in what triggers breeding between forest-living birds versus those of open country; we do not know the detailed trade-offs between underlying physiology, available food supply and immediate weather

conditions for any species. And yet where better to do this research?

Information exchange by birds at communal roosts is another topic originating from Singapore science, when it was noticed that birds roosting in big flocks (such as Yellow-vented Bulbuls, House Crows and Barn Swallows) appeared to follow others when leaving the roost and dispersing to seek out food the next morning. Were hungry birds that had low success the day before, following their more astute, chubbier and healthier colleagues back to known successful feeding sites? A lot of work has now gone into this topic around the world, but with few clear answers available yet.

Above: Looking vertically down into the deep cup-shaped nest of a Yellow-vented Bulbul (Pycnonotus goiavier) *reveals two glossy, speckled eggs; small clutches are typical.*

Opposite above: At larger scale, another downward view shows how building owners in the city are encouraged to create rooftop gardens that capitalize on under-utilized space to increase greenery.

Opposite below: Tree-clad gardens around colonial bungalows – some of them converted to small businesses, others residential – can be found side by side with skyscrapers in the city.

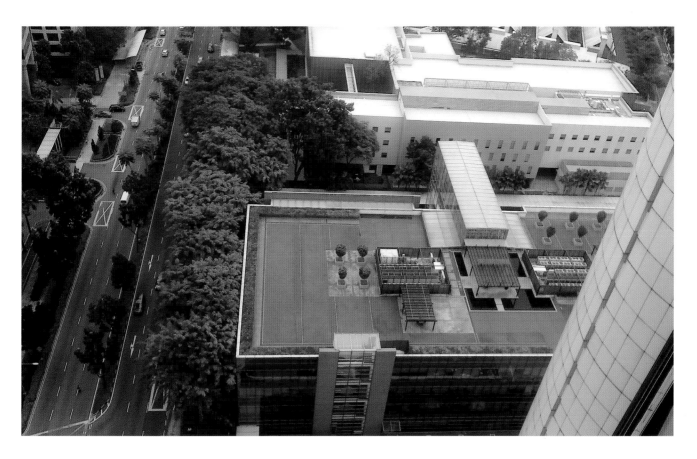

8
Woodlands and Secondary Vegetation

Wherever land is set aside, whether permanently or in the short term, a succession develops from grassland to scrub and so to secondary woodland. Often dominated by introduced trees such as rubber and *Acacia*, surprising discoveries can still be made there, including plants that had been thought lost decades ago, or even new records for Singapore. Secondary woodlands act as valuable extensions of natural and semi-natural habitat adding to the areas available for conservation and providing additional space for wildlife in and around the city.

Left: Native and exotic plants mingle to create scenery far removed from the idea of Singapore as a city with one of the world's highest-density populations.

Tampines Eco Green: secondary woodland in the eastern mainland of Singapore

It is interesting to compare the secondary woodland of Tampines Eco Green with the richness of the undisturbed rainforest at Bukit Timah. The trees are nearly all Earless Acacias (*Acacia auriculiformis*), which is an introduced species from the region of Papua New Guinea and Australia. Lying between these two giant land-masses is Thursday Island, in the Torres Strait, its original home. It's found throughout the region now, and could have been brought in centuries ago. The crescent-shaped leaves are not really leaves at all; they are expanded and flattened petiole-like structures called phyllodes. You can see an even more extreme example of this in the Black or Hickory Wattle (*Acacia mangium*), another introduced species that is spreading unpleasantly, but the seedlings have more typical feathery pinnate fronds.

They are pretty fire-resistant, and the seeds are even more resistant than the trees themselves. As the green pods ripen to brown they curl and split. Those tough phyllodes form a dry layer on the ground, hindering the growth of other plants; you can see that there is not much undergrowth here, and even grass does not do well beneath them. The dry layer burns easily, and without much competition the seeds lying in the surface soil will germinate easily and form another generation of *Acacia* trees. At Tampines Eco Green this is mitigated by the abundance of shallow ponds and waterlogged ground; elsewhere *Acacia* is often associated with hot, dry conditions with not many plants and yet not devoid of life either. Weaver Ants (*Oecophylla smaragdina*) form a great ball-nest up in the foliage, and if you put your hand on the trunk where they are moving, you will know all about it! That nest is woven together with sticky white thread, and it was Henry Ridley, the first Scientific Director of the Singapore Botanic Gardens, who discovered how the ants make it: they hold one of their own larvae gently in their jaws, dab it against one leaf, and pass it across to dab it against the next leaf, with its extruded gummy thread

making the link. Hundreds of ants doing this with hundreds or perhaps thousands of larvae will quickly build up a strong sticky net.

A good relationship

For any bird that can withstand the ants, these *Acacia* trees are pretty good perches though not great for food. All the common open country birds should be here: sunbirds, Collared Kingfishers, Spotted Doves and Zebra Doves (*Geopelia striata*), Pink-necked Green Pigeons (*Treron vernans*), bee-eaters and flycatchers, mynas, crows and cuckoos. You will find a woodpecker or two, and maybe even a nesting flyeater. Strictly speaking, that should now be called a Golden-bellied Gerygone (*Gerygone sulphurea*) – the books keep on changing the names. But one bird that really seems to specialize on the *Acacia* trees, in spite of the ants and almost certainly because of them, is the Baya Weaver (*Ploceus philippinus*).

Baya Weavers and *Acacia auriculiformis* don't naturally belong together because their historical ranges did not overlap. The male birds each make hanging nests from grass; you may see one bringing a long strip to his nest that is still green. As he continues, the plucked grass will turn yellow-

Opposite, clockwise from top left: The Banded Woodpecker (Picus miniaceus) *is a common resident of woodlands, excavating its nest hole in a dead tree-trunk; the spray of tiny yellow flowers of* Neptunia plena, *a common weed, opens sequentially from the tip to the base; many city parks contain areas of secondary vegetation interspersed with public facilities such as lawns, exercise tracks and sports fields; planted roadside trees are supplemented by those in gardens and private property as well as spontaneously regenerating woodland to create seamless greenery from the suburbs into the city centre.*

Mangroves
Freshwater, lakes & reservoirs
Lowland forest & secondary woodland

brown until it resembles the other nests in the colony. There may be ten or 15 of them in a little cluster of trees, which is a moderate-sized colony. The females can be distinguished because they lack yellow on their heads; they will be seen approaching half-completed nests, probably prospecting to adopt the best site and males therefore have to compete for her attention. Obviously it's important that this hanging nest should be strongly anchored and strongly built. It is protected from tree-climbing predators by the biting ants, but also it must not be attractive to the ants themselves. So there are plenty of things for a female to consider before she chooses.

The birds are probably taking a range of seeds from the local grasses as well as from the tall *Casuarina* trees – another fire-resistant species. You wouldn't expect to see a colony of weaverbirds in a solid grove of *Acacia*. Nests are typically placed in an isolated tree or in a small cluster of Acacias among other mixed vegetation. Predators find it harder to approach and are more easily spotted.

Right: The Weaver Ant folds leaves and glues them together using an exudate from its own larvae to create a nest.

Below: Smaller roads and junctions can be bridged by a nearly continuous canopy of tree crowns including those of Acacia, Rain Trees, figs *and many others.*

Green cover

A satellite image of Singapore taken in 1986 shows 37 per cent vegetation cover. A similar image taken in 2007 shows 46 per cent. Given the concurrent increase in land area owing to reclamation, the high population density and the demands of housing and transport, this seems a remarkable increase. It's partly explained because the word 'vegetation' includes every scrap of greenery from forest to roadside trees to football fields. Even newly reclaimed land beginning as bare soil or sand will quickly be covered by weeds such as Sensitive Plants (*Mimosa pudica*), *Neptunia* and Lallang Grass (*Imperata cylindrica*) that show up on images as vegetation.

Partly it's a matter of distortion by scale. Because Singapore is so small, with little natural forest remaining, roadside trees show up as a disproportionately large percentage of tree cover. The crowns of a row of big roadside trees can completely

Above: The Albizia (Albizia falcata) *is a quick-growing tree but this translates into soft and brittle wood that is easily snapped by a storm.*

Left: The smooth bark of Albizia *is decorated by a pattern of grey, white, green and rust-coloured lichens and algae.*

obscure the tarmac of a road beneath, so that on a satellite image portraying the visible surface, the land is classified as being vegetated. A patch of reclaimed land, though small, can be relatively large in percentage area terms, so inflating the numbers.

What the satellite images do show is the inevitability of reversion to greenery wherever land is left alone. Three vegetation types are particularly characteristic of Singapore though they can be found in various parts of South-East Asia. One is *Adinandra belukar* (*belukar* being the Malay term for secondary scrub); another is the parched woodland dominated by

introduced *Acacia*; and a third is the dense tangle over which tower *Albizia* trees. All three are secondary vegetation types that can follow when forest is completely removed. We encountered the *Adinandra* before in the coastal hill forest, as an inhabitant of very poor soils, and here it is the same story.

Above: Where it is allowed to grow unfettered, secondary woodland forms a dense mass of vegetation, less species-rich than the undisturbed forest but still valuable for plants and animals, and occasionally revealing surprising new records.

Adinandra

*A*cacia and *Adinandra* woodland are not unalike structurally, both being fairly small trees creating a species-poor mix of vegetation. Both are fire-prone. The soil is low in nitrogen and phosphorus, and acidic, limiting plant growth. The poverty of other species is striking, leading one to speculate whether the leaf litter from the dominant trees might contain growth inhibitors. No significant difference in foliar tannin concentrations has been found between secondary forest species from fertile versus those from nutrient-poor sites in Singapore.

However, the species typical of infertile sites have much tougher leaves that are difficult to break down. *Acacia* tends to grow at the edges of *Adinandra*-dominated stands, or in pure stands of its own where there has been landfill, compaction and levelling of the ground. *Acacia* carries relatively little interest for animals, but *Adinandra* attracts carpenter bees (*Xylocopus* spp.) for pollination and Lesser Dog-faced Fruit-bats for fruit dispersal. Once *Adinandra belukar* has developed, it seems not to develop further into more natural mixed forest, perhaps due to lack of a source for the seeds of other trees as much as the acidic and nutrient-poor conditions. But *Adinandra belukar* is now itself becoming scarce. This is not because it is naturally transient but because such areas are claimed for housing development. The best remaining examples are along the Southern Ridges at Mount Faber, Telok Blangah and Kent Ridge Parks, and on some of the offshore islands. *Adinandra belukar* also grows up on coastal bluffs where landslides take away the nutrient-rich topsoil and leave poor, hostile, red earth, and here are transitional types between *Adinandra belukar* and coastal forest.

Acacia

Although *Acacia* is a very large plant genus, with a huge distribution throughout the tropics and subtropics, only two were ever native to Singapore, both climbers now locally extinguished. *Acacias* generally seem to be adapted to more seasonal climates with a distinct dry season, and they cannot apparently invade the ever-wet tropical rainforest unless it is disturbed by man. Even then, they establish themselves only in the drier fringes, along logging tracks wide open to the sun or in big clearings, not amongst the dense vegetation. *Acacias* seem to suit poor soils, but dry ones. They probably have a competitive advantage on sun-baked poor soils due to the presence of nitrogen-fixing bacteria in root nodules, like many other members of the bean family.

Acacia auriculiformis has never been a significant source of timber, though it has probably been growing in Singapore for a couple of centuries. It doesn't form a well-shaped single main trunk, and the wood quality is poor. But it does form a significant part of the ecology of disturbed sites, which makes it all the more remarkable that it isn't even mentioned in standard text books like the *Tree Flora of Malaya*, or Whitmore's *Tropical Rain Forests*.

Below: The tiny yellow flowers of Acacia, with projecting stamens and reduced petals, are arranged along spike-like catkins and pollinated by flying insects.

Above: The Pacific Swallow (Hirundo tahitica) *is an aerial feeder over the top of the vegetation, and will often perch briefly on a bare twig; a moulting individual shows the glossier new blue-black feathers of back and wings gradually replacing the worn, older, brownish feathers.*

Opposite: Characteristic of mangroves, the Ashy Tailorbird (Orthotomus sepium) *has also invaded secondary woodland further away from the coast, where it flits rapidly about from twig to twig in the understorey as well as in trees such as the Ketapang* (Terminalia catappa).

Albizia

The third of the A's is *Albizia falcata* (sometimes known as *Paraserianthes falcataria*). Like the *Acacia*, this one is from eastern Indonesia, from the Moluccas but extending all the way to the Solomon Islands in the western Pacific. Here is a tree with a reputation, a pioneer that quickly colonizes open ground, but usually ground that is moister and less compacted than that preferred by the *Acacia*.

A kilogram (2.2 lb) of seeds can contain as many as 50,000 minute, easily wind-dispersed opportunities to colonize a new site. After they have ripened and the pods burst open, the seeds from any single tree will germinate over a long period, not all at the same time, so it's quite likely that some of the seeds will encounter good growing weather. And once they have started, do they grow! This is one of the fastest-growing trees in the world: in one experiment trees reached 16.45 m (54 ft) after only 20 months, with a girth of 33 cm (13 in), and the timber volume reached 80 cu m per hectare (1,130 cu ft per acre) of land. By ten years old, at the best sites, they have put on growth of 50 or 60 cu m per hectare (750 to 850 cu ft per acre) every year, though growth rates are highly sensitive to nutrients and may be halved on normal or poor soils.

In spite of being non-native, these trees are good for birds, good for insects and good for the understorey. They provide nest sites and perching sites for birds big and small, cavities for parakeets and woodpeckers, insect food for flycatchers, and they cast a dappled shade that is excellent for the growth of other saplings beneath them.

But here's the down side. Rapid growth means very light wood, less than 400 kg (900lb) per cubic metre, so it is weak and brittle. The trunk and larger branches are liable to snap in moderate winds, making it dangerous in public areas, and whole trees easily come down. Because it's a pioneer species, many individuals can establish themselves at one time, and they all tend to reach maturity and die at around the same time too, so that a piece of land that

Left: Poor growth form and a burden of epiphytes low on the trunk would never be permitted in a commercial rubber (Hevea brasiliensis) plantation, but can be tolerated in more ornamental surroundings.

Below: The trifoliate arrangement of rubber leaves is instantly recognisable; a short dry spell in January or February will trigger a change to orange and red followed by leaf fall and new foliage.

has not been a worry for years will suddenly face a succession of incidents. Throughout South-East Asia, municipal authorities are very wary of this tree.

Rubber

Those rubber plantations that Ridley did so much to encourage have left their mark. From the beginning of commercial estates in 1903, they covered nearly 40 per cent of Singapore by 1935, possibly the most widespread single land use ever. War, followed by the changing structure of the economy and competing uses for land, then led to a decline and the last commercial scale activities were probably in the 1960s and 1970s.

But the trees live on, propagating successfully with big three-seeded hard fruits that pop open explosively when ripe and heated by the sun. The seeds can be eaten, and possibly were, in times of economic hardship. Wild boars eat them, and so do squirrels. But these are seed predators that usually scrunch them up, not seed dispersers. Yet rubber trees can be found almost throughout Singapore, having been grown so widely. Any areas of secondary woodland, unless they have grown up after complete clearance and site preparation, are likely to house rubber trees. Rubber is abundant in the military areas that were once agricultural land with orchards and villages, and in the nature reserves. In its native Amazon rubber is a mid-layer tree of the rainforest, growing singly or in small numbers, and likewise in the forest-like conditions of secondary woodland in Singapore the seeds germinate quite successfully. Rubber will be here for a long time to come.

Opposite: Regenerating rubber forms a forest of thin, pole-sized trees with a lacy canopy that allows light to reach the ground, but the leaf litter can suppress the growth of other plants so that the understorey is sparse.

African tulip tree

'It seldom fruits in Malaya', said Corner about the African Tulip Tree (*Spathodea campanulata*), a statement that might take anyone by surprise today. This beautiful, pestilential tree seems to be everywhere, and its filmy silver seeds drift readily in the wind to colonize any unkempt ground. Presumably it was introduced because of its lovely flowers, bright orange-red, large and showy. These big cup-shaped blossoms are held upwards all over the top of the tree's crown, and, opening at around 4 a.m., are probably adapted for pollination by bats. Obviously the bat to which it may be adapted in its native West Africa is not present in Singapore, and the two or three nectar-feeding bats locally are much too scarce to be responsible for pollinating all the trees here.

More likely this is a generalist tree, capable of being pollinated by bats, moths, perhaps by big carpenter bees and by birds such as the Javan Mynas, Yellow-vented Bulbuls and Asian Glossy Starlings that visit the flowers and can be seen putting their whole heads into the bright 10-cm (4-in) cups. But did the local pollinators need to learn about the availability of nectar, or did they arrive later than the trees? Introduced Javan Mynas, for example, have only become common since the 1950s, later than the period of Corner's main Singapore experience, and perhaps it is they that have ensured the spread of this now abundantly fruiting tree.

Parade of the animals

These five examples of the commonest trees in secondary woodland present an interesting contrast in the pollination of their flowers and dispersal of their seeds. Several of them come from climates drier and more seasonal than that of Singapore, where the natural vegetation bears some resemblance to the secondary woodland here.

	Pollination	Dispersal
Adinandra	Carpenter bees	Bats
Acacia	Insects	Snapping pods, birds
Albizia	Insects	Wind
Hevea rubber	Insects	Exploding pods, animals
African Tulip	Bats, birds	Wind

Evidently they have differing strategies, which is not surprising given their different origins – only the *Adinandra* is native to Singapore – and it is interesting that one or two rely on wind for dispersal, because winds are typically light in this region. Wind is hardly used at all by trees of the mature primary rain forest with one notable exception: the bulky 'helicopter' seeds of dipterocarps.

Just as these trees are adaptable invaders of new sites, so the animals found with them are adaptable and mobile too. The rainforest specialists are unlikely to use such secondary growth unless it is adjacent to forest so that they can spread easily from one habitat to the other. Even then they might not find the specialized resources they require. So secondary woodland has the bulbuls and doves, the weaver birds and the Weaver Ants, the Plantain Squirrels (*Callosciurus notatus*) and nowadays the Wild Boar that can survive pretty much anywhere.

As a native plant, *Adinandra* is the one with its own native pollinators and dispersers. The animals that were associated with the introduced tree species have in general not accompanied them to their new home, but some others have arrived instead. Often these are introductions by people, often of animals that themselves come from more seasonal places. White-crested Laughingthrushes (*Garrulax leucolophus*), for example, are common cage-birds coming from Thailand, and escapees have established themselves since the mid 1990s. They do well in secondary woodland; how far they will penetrate into the true rainforest has still to be seen. Hwameis (*Garrulax canorus*) from China became established in the 1980s and now seem to be declining; Greater Necklaced Laughingthrushes (*Garrulax pectoralis*) were present from the 1970s but apparently seldom bred and may now have gone.

Above left: Flattened angular combs of the Honey Bee (Apis dorsata) *are sheltered from rain as they hang beneath boughs of Albizia. The openness of the foliage gives them a clear line of flight.*

Above right: A few common species of mammals predominate in secondary woodland, including the attractively striped and red-bellied Plantain Squirrel (Callosciurus notatus). *This is mainly a seed eater.*

A curiosity of old Singapore

Singapore is still divided administratively into mukims, a *mukim* being an old Malay term for a territorial area, an area served by a single mosque. Perhaps the nearest equivalent is the English parish. In 1936, 1 ha (2.5 acres) of sloping land in the mukim of South Seletar was purchased for $700 by Han Wai Toon, an immigrant from Hainan in China who had arrived in Singapore 21 years earlier. There, as described recently in a study by architect and historian Lai Chee Kien, Han intended to build his residence and to conduct agricultural experiments.

In 1936 this was not a forest site. It was partly covered with the invasive, fire-resistant grass known as Lallang (*Imperata cylindrica*), with scrub and old plantations. Its precise history before 1936 is unclear, but it had probably been subject to a succession of agricultural uses after the clearance of forest for gambier cultivation, and then pepper, pineapple or rubber, or some combination of these. Han, a broadly and deeply self-educated pioneer, was of the view that such degraded land could be returned to agricultural production. He cleared all vegetation and roots and burnt them, together with whatever humus layer existed, so as to produce an ash layer. He introduced terraces following the contour lines, and along each of these at surprisingly long intervals of 10 to 12 m (33 to 39 ft) he prepared planting mounds a few centimetres high. These were used to plant out 200 Rambutan trees (*Nephelium lappaceum*), though Han had other crops as well. The purpose of the mounds was to add nutrients and prevent the roots of the young trees from being flooded. Fallen leaf litter, twigs and fruit were raked up around the bases of the trees to maintain the mounds and to act as fertilizer.

This tranquil place became a haven for scholars, writers and artists, both locally born and visiting mainland Chinese, many of whom were members of the literary South Seas Society that had been co-founded by Han. A quarter of a century later, however, after the construction of Upper Thomson Road, a circuit was created in 1961 for the Singapore Grand Prix that encircled his estate. Han's estate was sold in 1962 when he returned to China to take up an advisory post on ceramics, but it would be no surprise if noisy car racing and crowds disturbing the peace of his orchard encouraged him to leave. The grand prix events for sports cars, vintage cars and motorcycles attracted more than a quarter of a million visitors in peak years.

The estate then became a chicken farm; other chicken and pig farms run by settlers from Hainan were already present in the surrounding area. The car racing circuit followed what is now Upper Thomson Road on one side and Old Upper Thomson Road on the other, but racing ceased in 1973. From being a mixed agricultural and recreational area, 40 years later the site has now grown into tall secondary forest. The spring that supplied water to the Rambutan orchard is still present in the valley between these two roads, and bits of metalwork and fragments of old jars can still be found in places.

Above: *The Little Bronze Cuckoo* (Chrysococcyx minutillus) *– the red skin round the eye identifies this as a male – is a common but easily overlooked resident of coastal forest, mangroves and secondary woodland.*

Opposite: *Having lost most of the original primary forest in the 19th century, Singapore values secondary woodland as a supplement for conservation purposes; with different plant species it mimics the original forest structure.*

They are embedded within rich, damp, black topsoil that has developed over what had been completely burnt over in 1936 and probably cleared again, but patchily, in the 1960s.

9
Singapore's Wild Future

The small size of Singapore and the intensity of development pose great challenges for nature conservation. An increasingly sophisticated and engaged human population demands that the environment must be well cared for, and methods for wildlife management must respond. Networking between protected areas with corridors, overhead wildlife bridges, species reintroductions and long-term monitoring are all being put in place. The Singapore Index of Cities' Biodiversity, a tool for international use, is being employed as a measurement of the wellbeing of biological diversity in this city state.

Left: High-rise living makes it possible to devote space to nature, important for recreation, enjoyment and many other environmental benefits from parks and nature reserves.

Species

In a territory as small as that of Singapore, it's inevitable that the population size of each species is small. And a single change in land use, because it occupies a relatively large area, will have a greater impact on the plant and animal populations than would a similarly sized development in a bigger country. Less than half a per cent of the country supports primary forest. Thirty per cent of plant species have been locally extirpated, and only 11 per cent of the original native flora consists of species that are still ranked as common. Among the butterflies only 141 out of the surviving 298 species (just 37 per cent of the 381 species ever recorded) are classified as common or moderately common.

On the other hand there is a steady flow of descriptions of new species, and new records of species already described from elsewhere, either because they have always been here but were overlooked, or because they have newly arrived by natural colonization.

Every one of these changes poses a dilemma, whether it is a loss or a potential loss that should be prevented, or a new discovery. With an increasing human population it is unlikely that conservation will become easier, and every bit of land and sea area counts. Small populations and small areas of habitat mean that the possibility of chance extinctions is high even with conservation measures in place. 'Relaxation' of the plant and animal communities by the drop-out of species following reduction in area of ecosystems is a long-term process, so reductions in area during the 19th century will have had inevitable consequences such that extinctions must be in progress now and will continue inevitably into the future. One role of conservation is to minimize these losses and reverse them when possible.

Right: White-bellied Sea-eagles (Haliaeetus leucogaster) *have taken to nesting on telecoms towers even close to buildings; the adults supply fish and bring fresh nest material too.*

Above: At Sungei Buloh Wetland Reserve, migrant Whimbrels (Numenius phaeopus) *roost in the mangroves at high tide when the mudflats are inundated.*

Opposite below: The Blue Pansy (Junonia orithya) *is abundant on the very short grass of lawns and roadside verges.*

Above: The Tawny Coster (Acraea violae) *is a recent arrival in Singapore, having spread down the Malay Peninsula as land was opened up for agriculture.*

Left: Lesser Grass Blue (Zizina otis): *more than one third of Singapore's extant butterflies – 106 out of 298 – are members of the Family Lycaenidae.*

Endemism

Nobody can tell you how many endemic species Singapore has. The flowering plants (three endemics, two of them extinct) and ferns (no endemics) are quite well known, but the invertebrate animals and all kinds of marine animals are known rather poorly. A few endemic species, like the Freshwater Crab (*Johora singaporensis*), have been profiled as species for which Singapore has a special and global responsibility, but there are many others less well known. Among the more than 150 new species of flies described from Singapore in the past decade, many are known only from Singapore, some of them only from a single specimen, and for the moment they have to be considered endemic, but it is currently impossible to tell how many of them might occur in the neighbouring regions too. Even some marine crabs are known only from Singapore waters, and these are perhaps even more likely to be present but overlooked along the adjacent coasts of Malaysia or Indonesia.

Above: *Gapis (*Saraca declinata*) is a native riverside tree that has been used extensively for urban planting; it flowers on the branches and even the trunk, and is popular with many insects.*

Left: *Another plant attracting many insects is the Coral Vine* (Antigonon leptopus), *but this is an introduced species used for fencing and hedging. It often draws large numbers of Stingless Bees* (Trigona *spp.).*

Above: *Lesser Whistling Ducks* (Dendrocygna javanica) *are quite mobile, staying on ponds in parks and rural areas by day, and apparently moving extensively by night.*

Left: *Mangrove creeks provide adventure and education for young people: an excellent introduction to nature in Singapore that will help to motivate the next generation.*

What makes Singapore special?

In this sense Singapore is little different from other tropical cities; the scale and intensity of research has varied a great deal over time, from place to place and between different animal groups; and the patchiness of information is highlighted by the very detailed scale at which city planners work.

Nevertheless, some special features of Singapore are easy to identify. One is the proximity of wildlife to the city. Oriental Honey-buzzards, Greater Racket-tailed Drongos (*Dicrurus paradiseus*), Long-tailed Parakeets, Hill Mynas (*Gracula religiosa*) and Oriental Pied Hornbills can all be encountered in or near the city centre. Several of these are scarce or at risk in the South-East Asian region because they rely on lowland forest that is rapidly being converted to plantation agriculture, yet at least three of them (Greater Racket-tailed Drongos, Long-tailed Parakeets, Hill Mynas) are able to survive in Singapore's parks because they rely on the taller trees

and the condition of the lower storey vegetation has little relevance to them. Common Palm-civets and Reticulated Pythons are other examples of wildlife that manage to live near people, sometimes in harmony and sometimes not.

Some international rarities reach an end point on their migrations in Singapore. Himalayan Griffon Vultures (*Gyps himalayensis*) have been seen over the main shopping district in Orchard Road, and internationally endangered birds like the Spoon-billed Sandpiper (*Eurhinorhynchus pygmaeus*) as well as a widespread Eurasian migrant such as the Northern Shoveler (*Anas clypeata*) have reached their southernmost point here in Singapore.

The Red-legged Crake (*Rallina fasciata*) is a weird example of a species that is extremely difficult to spot anywhere because of its intensely shy behaviour. It tends to be active early in the morning or at dusk, and keeps to swampy vegetation. Yet in Singapore Botanic Gardens these attractive birds can sometimes be seen wandering about in the open, amongst the

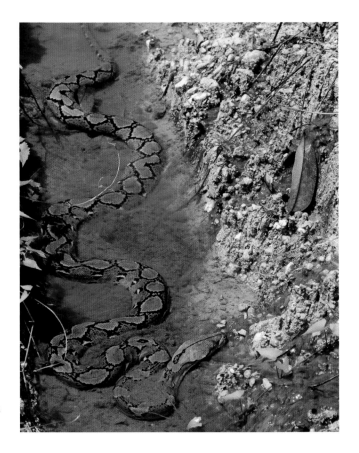

Left: Natural recolonization by Oriental Pied Hornbills (Anthracoceros albirostris) *has been facilitated by providing nest boxes for wild birds, though natural cavities are still preferred. The female and young will break out of the mud-sealed entrance after about 90 days.*

Below: Rats are likely to form the main prey of the surprisingly common Reticulated Python (Malayopython reticulatus), *a snake that is fond of water.*

flower beds, and occasionally just a few metres away from people walking their dogs.

Some rarities are doing better in Singapore than anywhere else. Great-billed Herons, Straw-headed Bulbuls (*Pycnonotus zeylanicus*) and Grey-headed Fish-eagles have all built up notable populations and can be located by any birdwatcher who visits the right habitat. This situation is due, presumably, to a combination of reduced pressures (such as minimization of poaching) and even the provision of unnatural or semi-natural resources (such as reservoirs and introduced fish).

Undisturbed reefs and seagrass beds provide important marine habitat. In 2011 container traffic reached 29.94 million units, and gross tonnage of shipping entering and leaving Singapore reached 2.12 billion tonnes. So far, spillages and collisions have thankfully been rare and on a small scale. Diversity of ecosystems within a small area is a key point about the Singapore environment – it is possible to reach coral reefs, lowland dipterocarp forest and mangroves all within an hour of each other, and within reach of an electricity supply, research institutes and high-tech laboratory facilities. The high proportion of land under military use offers a significant level of de facto protection to wildlife.

Singapore provides opportunities for experiment and the development of unusual techniques, such as integrated nestboxes for hornbills, growth and nutrition experiments with corals, and physical trials with mangrove restoration techniques. There are also opportunities for natural recolonization by plants and animals that have previously been lost: porcupines, Large Indian Civet, Sambar Deer, Wild Boar and Red Junglefowl (*Gallus gallus*) are all recent examples.

Below: The Nature Society (Singapore) has motivated properties along Orchard Road to plant up their land with vegetation to form a Butterfly Trail that within a year has already increased diversity of species

Putting a framework in place

As part of the activities surrounding the build-up to the Rio de Janeiro UN Conference on Environment and Development, in 1992 government produced a document called the Singapore Green Plan. The 1992 Conference formed an array of international agreements: the Convention on Biological Diversity (CBD), the UN Framework Convention on Climate Change (UNFCCC), and the UN Convention to Combat Desertification (UNCCD). Singapore has signed all of these. Also put in place was a process leading to the UN Forum on Forests (UNFF), in which all UN member countries are de facto participants. Singapore is also a signatory to the Convention on International Trade in Endangered Species of Flora and Fauna (CITES).

The 1992 Singapore Green Plan was a ten-year plan (1992–2001), succeeded by the 2011 Singapore Green Plan (2002–2011) and now by the Singapore Sustainability Blueprint. Meanwhile, a Singapore Blue Plan addressing the marine environment has been put forward by academics and members of the non-governmental community.

Under the UN Framework Convention on Climate Change, Singapore has developed through public, government and industry consultation a National Climate Change Strategy that is available on-line. Under the Convention on Biological Diversity, Singapore has developed a National Biodiversity Strategy and Action Plan, also available on-line.

Putting these into effect cannot be the responsibility of any single government agency, or even of government as a whole. Public consultation is required at nearly every level, including the formulation of the ten-yearly Concept Plans and the five-yearly Master Plans. It is under the Concept Plan that the broad thrust of land use patterns is determined, with the details filled in by the Master Planning process. Singapore is proud of its record in greening the city since independence in 1965, and the Garden City concept has been subtly transformed into City In A Garden, a city that is embedded within a garden nation. There is still a lot of 'wild' in Singapore, but the reality is that this is a densely populated and intensively managed nation.

It is tough to find realistic comparisons with Singapore as a city state. Monaco is tiny (1.5 sq km/ 0.6 sq miles) with no hinterland. Hong Kong is about double the area of Singapore, with a somewhat larger population, and has managed to set aside some 40 per cent of its land area in country parks, partly because the steep and unstable terrain has put a high cost on development beyond the main population centres. Luxembourg and Liechtenstein are entirely land-locked. Bahrain is very similar in size to Singapore, but has one tenth of the population and is intensely arid. Singapore is the only city state within the immediately equatorial humid tropical forest belt. The Singapore Index of Cities' Biodiversity was developed so that cities could assess their performance under the Convention on Biological Diversity. This Index is also available on-line. It is not meant to be a tool for comparison between cities, because there is little rationale for comparison in, say, species richness between Bucharest, Aden and Madras. It was designed as a tool for self-comparison over time, so that a particular city can make ball-park estimates of trends in biodiversity, conservation effort and public awareness.

Public awareness is becoming increasingly critical in developing policies that will ensure the sustainability of wild Singapore. Many current challenges, such as climate change, economic cycles and food security are determined by factors beyond the control of any single nation, and require to be addressed through global actions. Memories are short, and opinions tend to be formed by single striking events rather than by long-term statistical trends. One of these trends, however, is indeed towards increased public participation and demand for recreation, greenery and nature. School activities, volunteer programmes at nature reserves and internships for tertiary students add to the level of public engagement.

Left: Fragments of natural habitat within public parks ensure that these parks combine both recreational and conservation value, as at Admiralty Park with some rare freshwater swamp forest plants.

Opposite: As one of Singapore's most threatened ecosystems, freshwater swamp forest is mimicked by planting around lakes and ponds. Here massive pandans (Pandanus spp.) are fronted by Dillenia suffruticosa and backed by palms.

Pressures tell

Singapore's southern shores are dedicated to shipping, shipbuilding and other heavy industries. Despite massive world-class industrial facilities, nearby reefs and marine ecosystems remain rich. Since 1986, Singapore has been the busiest port in the world in terms of shipping tonnage, with an annual average of 140,000 vessel calls. At any one time, there are about 1,000 vessels in Singapore port. Singapore's container terminals line the southern mainland, handling about one-fifth of the world's total container transhipment. Singapore has more than 80 ship building and ship repair companies, holding about 70 per cent of the world's jack-up rig-building market and over 65 per cent of the global floating production storage and offloading conversion market. Most are found along the southern and southwestern coastline.

Singapore is among the world's three largest petrochemical refiners. Jurong Island, formed by reclamation of seven southern islands now has 95 petroleum, petrochemical and chemical companies with more than S$31 billion in fixed assets. Within weeks of declaring the reclamation of Jurong Island completed in September 2009, there were reports that further reclamation is being considered as land had run out on the island. Bukom Island is the site of Singapore's first oil refinery, set up in 1961 by Shell. Today, the 500,000 barrels-per-day Bukom Refinery is the largest Shell refinery in the world, in terms of crude distillation capacity, and 90 per cent of Bukom's products are exported. Singapore is also one of the top bunkering (ship refuelling) ports in the world. Annually, about 30 million tonnes (29.5 million tons) of bunkers are lifted in Singapore. This is enough to fill 12 thousand Olympic-sized pools.

Much of Singapore's reefs have been affected by land reclamation and coastal development. Singapore once had over 60 offshore islands and patch reefs. However, since the 1970s, major land reclamation has merged many islands and reef flats. These works have not only reduced live coral coverage by about

Opposite: The inevitable effects of land reclamation are managed by an environmental impact assessment procedure and strict enforcement, so that Singapore's practices have been featured in international scientific literature.

Right: Living with nature requires compromises that are not unique to any one country: neither environmental problems nor solutions are limited by political boundaries but here industry, recreation and nature can fit together.

65 per cent since the 1980s, but also resulted in murky waters which reduced sunlight penetration from 10 m (33 ft) in the 1960s to about 2 m (6 ft 6 in) today. Nevertheless, Singapore's remaining reefs still harbour nearly 200 species of hard corals and a good variety of other marine life.

It's a similar story on land. Demand for land is not getting less, and strong justifications are needed for retaining nature. Singapore ranks among the top five offshore financial centres in the world, depending on the measure used, and it has the world's highest density of wealthy people, with over 150,000 individuals (2.95 per cent of the population) having net worth of US$1 million or more. But the affluent and the less affluent require greenery and nature. It is easy to mock new concepts such as 'nature deficit disorder', but the fact is that demand for access to nature has never been stronger in Singapore than it is today. Conservation of wild Singapore is therefore an issue for government planners and for non-governmental organizations, as well as for resource-dependent industries that cannot afford to lose their resource base and cannot be seen to do one thing in Singapore and another thing overseas.

Most current conservation activities are done in conjunction between government and the public, and many are led or initiated by the non-governmental community, such as planning for use of the former railway corridor as green space, greening of a butterfly corridor down Orchard Road, with further contributions by publications, websites, guided tours, surveys and monitoring of a wide range of plants and animals.

As is the case elsewhere in South-East Asia, the story of environmental loss over the past two centuries has not been a happy one. These losses occurred through the extraction of natural resources for economic gain. Now, however, economic gain has led to the emergence of an affluent nation and higher standards of living for citizens who call for the better management and conservation of those very same resources.

Resources

Acknowledgements

Mr Poon Hong Yuen, the CEO of the National Parks Board (NParks) at the time this book was first published, and Deputy CEO of NParks, Dr. Leong Chee Chiew, made arrangements enabling us to produce this book. We wish to thank Wong Tuan Wah, Lena Chan, Elaine Phua, Grace Ng, Lee Pin Pin, Ng Li-San, Germaine Ong and Emmalyn Lai for their assistance. Staff of the Library, Singapore Botanic Gardens, as well as Lim Wei Ling provided help with photographs.

Much marine life is cryptic and was found by experienced shore explorers who include Toh Chay Hoon, Marcus Ng, James Koh, Loh Kok Sheng and Neo Mei Lin. Thanks also to the Raffles Museum of Biodiversity Research for identification and for including us in scientific field trips, and Neo Mei Lin for allowing us to be part of her field work which took us to some special shores.

Some of the statistics are derived from information from Prof. Richard Corlett and Prof. Chou Loke Ming. Information on particular topics was derived from work by Andie Ang and Mirza Rifqi Ismail (Banded Leaf-monkeys), and by Robin Ngiam Wen Jiang (dragonflies). We gratefully acknowledge the Singapore Biodiversity Encyclopedia (Ng et al. 2011) as a tremendous source of information, and express our thanks to those who are listed in the bibliography as sources of biological and historical facts – for example the stories of Han Wai Toon (Lai 2011) and of Wallace's correspondence (van Wyhe & Rookmaker 2011). Information on Singapore land areas, development, population, industry and shipping was taken from websites and publications that are all in the public domain.

Bibliography

Buckley, C.B. 1902, *An Anecdotal History of Old Times in Singapore*, 1819–1867. Fraser & Neave, Singapore.

Chong, K.Y., Tan, H.T.W. and Corlett, R.T. 2009, *A Checklist of the Total Vascular Plant Flora of Singapore: Native, Naturalised and Cultivated Species*. Raffles Museum of Biodiversity Research, National University of Singapore, Singapore. Uploaded 12 November 2009. *http://rmbr.nus.edu.sg/raffles_museum_pub/flora_of_singapore_tc.pdf*

Collis, M. 1968. *Raffles: the definitive biography*. Faber and Faber, London.

Corner, E.J.H. 1949, The durian theory or the origin of the modern tree. *Annals of Botany*, New Series, 13: 367–414.

Corner, E.J.H. 1964, *The Life of Plants*. Weidenfeld and Nicholson, London.

Corner, E.J.H. 1978, *The Freshwater Swamp-forest of South Johore and Singapore*. Gardens' Bulletin, Supplement No. 1. Singapore.

Corner, E.J.H. 1988, *Wayside Trees of Malaya*, Vols. 1 and 2. 3rd edition. Malayan Nature Society, Kuala Lumpur.

Darwin, C. and Wallace, A.R. 1858, On the tendency of species to form varieties; and on the perpetuation of varieties and species by natural means of selection. *Journal and Proceedings of the Linnean Society: Zoology*, 3(9): 45–52.

Davies, R. 2012, How Charles Darwin received Wallace's Ternate paper 15 days earlier than he claimed: a comment on van Wyhe and Rookmaker (2012) [sic]. *Biological Journal of the Linnean Society*, 105: 472–477.

Hornaday, W.T. 1885, *Two Years in the Jungle: The Experiences of a Hunter and Naturalist in India, Ceylon, the Malay Peninsula and Borneo*. Charles Scribner's Sons, New York.

Kathirithamby-Wells, J. 2005, *Nature and Nation. Forests and Development in Peninsular Malaysia*. NIAS Press, Denmark.

Khew, S.K. 2010, *A Field Guide to the Butterflies of Singapore*. Ink On Paper, Singapore.

Lai, C.K. 2011. Rambutans in the picture: Han Wai Toon and the articulation of space by the Overseas Chinese in Singapore. Pp. 151–172 in Heng, D. and Syed Muhd. Khairudin Aljuneid (eds.), *Singapore in Global History*. ICAS/Amsterdam University Press, Amsterdam.

McKenzie, L.J. (2008), Seagrass Educators Handbook, Seagrass-Watch HQ. Cairns. 20pp. [1.3Mb] *http://www.seagrasswatch.org/Info_centre/education/Seagrass_Educators_Handbook.pdf*

National Biodiversity Strategy and Action Plan. *http://www.cbd.int/doc/world/sg/sg-nbsap-v2-en.pdf*

National Biodiversity Strategy and Action Plan. *www.nparks.gov.sg/cms/docs/nbc/NPark-booklet-final-4sep.pdf*

National Climate Change Strategy. *http://app.mewr.gov.sg/data/ImgUpd/NCCS_Full_Version.pdf*

National Heritage Board. 2012. Yesterday.sg. *http://yesterday.sg/discover-more/communities-festivals/communities/the-malays /* Accessed 4 Jan 2012

Ng, P.K.L., Corlett, R.T. and Tan, H.T.W. 2011, *Singapore Biodiversity. An Encyclopedia of the Natural Environment and Sustainable Development*. Editions Didier Millet, Singapore.

Oliver, G., Zaw, K. and Hotson, M. 2011, Dating rocks in Singapore: plate tectonics between 280 and 200 million years ago. *Innovation*, 10: 22–25.

Ransonnet, E. von. 1876, *Skizzen aus Singapur und Djohor*, G. Westermann, Braunschweig. 88 pp. + i–xii, pls. 1–11, map. *http://sgebooks.nl.sg/details/020000189.html*

Singapore Index on Cities Biodiversity. *http://www.cbd.int/authorities/gettinginvolved/cbi.html*

Turner, I.M. 2011, *The Ecology of Trees in the Tropical Rain Forest*. Cambridge University Press, Cambridge.

van Wyhe, J. and Rookmaker, K. 2011, A new theory to explain the receipt of Wallace's Ternate Essay by Darwin in 1858. *Biological Journal of the Linnean Society*, 105: 249–252. For a contrary view see Davies (2012).

Wallace, A.R. 1855, On the law which has regulated the introduction of new species. *Annals and Magazine of Natural History*, 2nd Series, 16: 184–196.

Wallace, A.R. 1858, On the tendency of varieties to depart indefinitely from the original type. *Journal and Proceedings of the Linnean Society: Zoology*, 3(9): 53–62.

Wallace, A.R. 1869, *The Malay Archipelago: The land of the Orang-utan and the bird of paradise*. MacMillan, London.

Whitmore, T.C. 1984, *Tropical Rain Forests of the Far East*, 2nd edition. Oxford University Press, Oxford and London.

Index

Abdul Jalil IV, Bendahara
  Sultan 18
Abdu'r Rahman, Dato'
  Temenggong Sri Maharaja 18
Acacia, Earless 176
Acacia spp. 169, 175, 178, 180,
  181, 186
  auriculiformis 12, 176, 181
  mangium 176
Acraea violae 193
Acridotheres javanicus 156, 163
  tristis 156, 158
Acropora corals 83
Acrostichum aureum 11
Adinandra spp. 130, 169, 180,
  186
  belukar 179, 180, 181
Admiralty Park 198
Aegithina tiphia 136
Aeschynanthus spp. 151
Aetobatus narinari 79
Albizia falcata 179, 180, 183, 186
  saman 15, 21, 160
Alcedo atthis 140
  meninting 142
Alcyoniidae Family 77, 85
Alder, White 166
Alphonso, Arthur 30
Amaurornis phoenicurus 170
Amazon waterlily 27, 29
Amphidromus atricallosus 151
Amphiprion ocellaris 85
Anas clypeata 195
Anemone, Giant Carpet 85
  Lined Bead 64
Anemonefish, False Clown 85
Anisoptera megistocarpa 119
Anomalosiphon murphyi 152
Ant, Weaver 176, 178, 187
Anthracoceros albirostris 104,
  196
Anthus rufulus 170
Antigonon leptopus 194
Api-api Jambu 96
Api-api Putih 93
Apis dorsata 187
Aplonis panayensis 159
Arachnoides placenta 73
Archaster typicus 75
Archer Fish, Banded 88
Arctitis binturong 18
Ardea cinerea 56, 103, 140
  purpurea 138
  sumatrana 56, 87

Arnold, Thomas 18
Ashtoret lunaris 77
Asplenium nidus 112
Atherinomorus duodecimalis
  85
Avicennia spp. 93, 96
  alba 93
  marina 96

Baccaurea spp. 116
Bakau 93
Bakau Mata Buaya 91
Balaenoptera edeni 60
Bambusa vulgaris 31
Bannerman, Colonel 17
Barringtonia racemosa 24
Bat, Cave Nectar 100
  House 167
Bee, Carpenter 114, 180
  Honey 187
  Stingless 194
Bee-eater, Blue-tailed 136
  Blue-throated 130, 133
Binturong 18
Bird, Weaver 187
Bittern, Cinnamon 136
  Yellow 136, 138
bladderwort 170
Boar, Wild 4, 41, 50, 51, 119,
  128, 197
Boleophthalmus boddarti 107
Botanic Gardens, Singapore
  30, 31, 33, 48, 176
Bronchocela cristatella 4, 15,
  158
Bronzeback, Red-necked 15
Brooke, James 15
Bruguiera spp. 93
  gymnorrhiza 94
  hainesii 91
  parviflora 95
Bubulcus ibis 159
Bucida molineti 165
Bukit Puaka 23
Bukit Timah 23, 31, 39, 127
  Nature Reserve 16, 47,
  112-14, 115, 128, 139
Bukom Island 200
Bulbophyllum macranthum
  151
Bulbul, Straw-headed 196
  Yellow-vented 159, 162, 166,
  170, 172, 186
Bullfrog, American 139

Bulrush, Cat-tail 156, 165, 166
Burkill, I.H. 17, 30
Burmannia coelestis 170
Bush-frog, Blue-spotted 151
Buta-buta 90
Butterflyfish, Copperband 80
Butterfly Trail 197, 201

Cacomantis merulinus 136
  sepulcralis 136
Calliphara nobilis 90
Callosciurus notatus 187
Calotes versicolor 167
Canavalia cathartica 146
Canna indica 145, 156
  generalis 165
Canna Lily 165
Canna, Water 145, 156
Cantley, Nathaniel 17, 30, 31
Caprimulgus macrurus 167
Carcinoscorpius rotundicauda
  99
carpenter bees 49
Casmerodius albus 56, 138
Casuarina spp. 178
Catcher, Housefly 165
cave corals 82
Central Catchment Nature
  Reserve 47, 120, 128, 152
Ceratosoma sinuatum 78
Cerberus rynchops 97, 108,
  109
Ceriagrion cerinorubellum 143
Ceriops tagal 109
  zippeliana 109
Cervus unicolor 41, 51
Chaetodermis penicilligerus 72
Changi 66, 70, 75
Changi Point 4, 29
Chasen, F.N. 17, 33, 149
Chek Jawa 45, 56, 72, 75, 103,
  104
Chelmon rostratus 80
Chelonia mydas 76
Cherry, Malayan 166
Chew Wee Lek 30
Chin See Chung 30
Chlidonias leucopterus 138
Chromide, Green 88
Chromodoris lineolata 79
Chrysococcyx minutillus 188
Chyrosopelea genus 125
Cinnamomum iners 26, 160
Cinnamon 26, 160

Cinnyris jugularis 158, 159
Civet, Common Palm 18, 169,
  195
  Large Indian 128. 197
Claoxylon indicum 145
Cliona patera* 61, 76
Clubmoss 169
Coccinea grandis 147
Coleman, George 18
Colugo 124, 125
Columba livia 156
Congrogadus subducens 85
Copsychus malabaricus 112
  saularis 168
Coral, Castle 82
Coral Crab, Red 82
coral 54, 80-3
  bleaching 83
  mass spawning 84-5
Coraltail, Ornate 143
Cordia cylindristachys 166
Corner, John 17, 30, 144, 145,
  146, 148, 186
Corvus splendens 156
Coster, Tawny 193
Cosymbotus craspedotus 125
Crab, Johnson's Freshwater
  139, 151
  Singapore Freshwater 139,
  194
  Swamp Forest 139
  Tree Climbing 97
Crake, Red-legged 195
Cratoxylum cochinchinense
  133
Crawfurd, John 25
Crocodile, Estuarine 88
  Saltwater 50
Crocodylus porosus 50, 88
Crow, House 156, 159, 172
Cryptelytrops purpureomaculatus
  97, 108, 109
Cuckoo, Little Bronze 188
  Plaintive 136
  Rusty-breasted 136
Cuthona sibogae 79
Cymbidium finlaysonianum
  151
Cymbiola nobilis 72
Cynodon dactylon 170
Cynopterus brachyotis 167, 168
Cyornis rufigastra 104
Cypraea ovum 68

Cyrene Reef 54-6, 72, 75
Cyrtophyllum fragrans 33
Cyrtostachys renda 148

Dairy Farm Nature Park 16, 127
Darwin, Charles 12
Deer, Sambar 41, 51, 128, 197
Dendrelaphis kopsteini 15
Dendrobium crumenatum 40, 41
Dendrocopos moluccensis 156
Dendrocygna javanica 136, 156, 195
Dendrophylliidae Family 82

Diadumene lineata 64
Diaenia ophrydis 151
Dicrurus paradiseus 195
Dillenia suffruticosa 49, 136, 170, 171, 198
Dinopium javanense 136
Dipteris conjugata 130
Dipterocarpaceae Family 115, 116
Dipterocarpus grandiflorus 112
    tempehes 117
Doleschallia bisaltide 136
Dolphin, Bottle-nosed 60
    Indo-Pacific Hump-backed 60
Dove, Red Turtle 136
    Spotted 136, 159, 176
    Zebra 176
Draco melanopogon 114, 124
    quinquefasciatus 124
    sumatranus 112, 124
Dragon, Blue 78, 79
Drill 64
Drongo, Greater Racket-tailed 195
Duck, Whistling 136, 156, 195
Dugong 70, 72
Dugong dugon 70
Dungun 90
Durian 100, 122
Durian Theory 146, 148
Durio zibethinus 122
Dwarf Geometry Tree 165

Echinosorex gymnurus 18
Eel-blenny, Carpet 85
Eggfly, Great 166
Egret, Cattle 159, 170
    Great 56, 138, 140
    Little 140, 159, 171
Egretta garzetta 140, 171
Elaeocarpus ferrugineus 124
Elephant, Asian 51

Elphas maximus 51
Enhalus acoroides 53
Enigmonia aenigmatica 97
Episesarma spp. 97, 107
Eonycteris spelaea 100
Eretmochelys imbricata 76
Eriphia ferox 63
Etroplus suratensis 88
Eudynamys scolopacea 156
Eurema blanda 136
Eurhinorhynchus pygmaeus 195
Eutropis multifasciatus 127
Excoecaria agallocha 90

Falco peregrinus 101, 162
Falcon, Peregrine 101, 162
Farquhar, William 17, 25
Fern, Bird's Nest 112
    Mangrove 11
Ficus religiosa 160, 162
fiddler crab 107, 108
Fig, Bodhi 162
Filefish, Feathery 72
Fish-eagle, Grey-headed 50, 136, 140, 196
Flameback, Common 136
Flycatcher, Asian Brown 136
    Mangrove Blue 104
Flying Dragon, Black-bearded 114
    Five-banded 124
    Sumatran 124
flying fox 33
Forest Reserves map 31
Fort Canning 18, 19, 21, 23, 25
Fruit-bat, Lesser Dog-faced 167, 168, 180

Galaxea spp. 81
Galeopterus variegatus 124
Gallinago gallinago 170
    stenura 170
Gallirallus striatus 170
Gallus gallus 197
Gambusia affinis 139
Gapis 194
Gardens By The Bay 48
Garrulax canorus 187
    leucolophus 187
    pectoralis 187
Gecko, Brown's Flap-legged 125
    Frilly 125
    House 158
    Kuhl's Gliding 125
Gelam 156
Geopelia striata 176

Gerygone, Golden-bellied 176
Gerygone sulphurea 176
Gobiodon histrio 83
Goby, Broad-barred Acropora 83
Gracula religiosa 195
Grapsus albolineatus 67
Grass Blue, Lesser 193
Grass, Lallang 179, 187
Greenshank 90, 99
Grenadier, Scarlet 153
Gyps himalayensis 195

Halcyon smyrnensis 140, 143
Haliaeetus leucogaster 50, 136, 192
Haliastur indus 156
Halophila decipiens 101
Hamilton, Captain Alexander 18
Han Wai Toon 187, 188
Hawk-eagle, Changeable 50, 136
Hemidactylus frenatus 158
Henderson, Murray 30
Heritiera littoralis 90
Heron, Great-billed 56, 87, 196
    Grey 56, 103, 140
    Purple 138, 140
Hevea brasiliensis 33, 184, 186
Hibiscus rosa-sinensis 156
Hirundo rustica 133, 171
    tahitica 183
Holttum, Richard 17, 30, 33
Honey-buzzard, Oriental 50, 51, 162, 195
Hornaday, William 60, 61
Hornbill, Oriental Pied 104, 195, 196
Horsburgh Lighthouse 57, 59, 103
Horseshoe Crab, Coastal 99
    Mangrove 99
Horsfield, Thomas 18
House-shrew 158
Hoya verticillata 24
Hwamei 187
Hymenopus coronatus 168
Hypolimnas bolina 166
Hypothymis azurea 104
Hystrix brachyura 128

Ichthyophaga ichthyaetus 50, 136
Idioctis littoralis 98
Imperata cylindrica 179, 187

Irmengardia johnsoni 139
Ironwood 33
Isognomon ephippium 97
    isgonomon 64
Istana, the 26
Ixobrychus cinnamomeus 136
    sinensis 136, 138
Ixora javanica 156

Jack, William 17, 22, 60, 130
Jingle Clam, Mangrove 97
Johor 43, 50
Johor River 63, 72
Johor Straits 44, 63, 104, 130
Johora singaporensis 139, 194
Julidan millipedes 127
Junglefowl, Red 197
Junonia orithya 166, 192
Jurong 23, 45, 145, 146
Jurong forest 146
Jurong Island 35, 54, 56, 200
Jurong Lake 142
Jurong Central Park 156-8

Kembang Semangkok 123
Kemutong 133
Keruing Belimbing 112
Ketapang 183
Khaya grandifolia 156
Kingfisher, Blue-eared 142
    Collared 133, 140, 156, 176
    Common 140
    Stork-billed 142
    White-throated 140, 143
Kite, Brahminy 156
Kloss, Boden 17, 33
Koel, Asian 156
Kogia breviceps 60
Kopsia singapurensis 48, 151
Kopsia, White-flowered 151
Kranji Reservoir 138
Kwan Koriba, Professor 30, 148

Labrador 66
    Nature Reserve 47
Laganum depressum 73
Lalage nigra 136
Lallang 179, 187
Lapwing, Red-wattled 170
Lates calcarifer 59
Lathrecista asiatica 153
Laticauda colubrina 84
Laughingthrush, Greater Necklaced 187
    White-crested 187
Leaf, Autumn 136
Leaf-monkey, Banded 123,

135, 146, 149
Silvered 18
Leban 114
Leopard Cat 128
Ligia spp. 68
exotica 66
Liparis ferruginea 170
lipstick flower 151
Livia subviridis 88
Lizard, Changeable 167
Flying 112
Green Crested 4, 15, 158
Loras, Common 136
Lorikeet, Rainbow 158
Ludwigia octovalvis 147
Luperosaurus browni 125
Lutrogale perspicillata 51, 95, 101, 105
Lycaenidae Family 138, 193
Lycopodiella cernuum 169

Macaca fascicularis 18, 112, 120
nemsestrina 145
Macaque, Long-tailed 18,112, 120, 122, 169
Pigtailed 145
Macaranga gigantea 119, 147, 148
MacRitchie Reservoir 142
Macrobrachium brachyteles 151
Magpie-robin, Oriental 168
Mahang, Giant 119, 147, 148
Mahogany, African 156
Malacca Straits of 39
Malayopython reticulatus 50, 196
Mandai 23, 45, 91, 119, 146
Mangrove Spider, Hairy-foot 98
mangroves 43, 86-109
Manis javanica 168, 169
Mantis, Orchid 168
Martin, William 149
Melaleuca cajuputi 156
Melastoma malabathricum 4, 166
Mempoyan 130
Menasi 112
Merops philippinus 136
viridis 130, 133
Merremia hederacea 149
Mesua ferrea 33
Metopograpsus spp. 66
Mimosa pudica 179
Monarch, Black-naped 104
Monitor, Water 88, 108
Monitor Lizard 139

Mood Crab, Spotted 77
moon snails 75
Moonrat 18
Mosquitofish 139
Moss, Climbing 151
Moth, Wall Bagworm 163
Mouse-Deer, Lesser 41, 128
mud lobster 98
Mudskipper, Bearded 107
Blue-spotted 107
Giant 106, 107
Yellow-spotted 106
mudskippers 106-7
Mullet, Greenback 88
Munshi Abdullah 18
Murton, Henry 30
Muscicapa dauurica 136
Muntingia calabura 166
Myna, Common 156, 158, 159
Hill 194
Javan 156, 159, 163, 170, 172, 186

Naticidae Family 75
National Parks Board 46
Nee Soon 139, 144, 148, 149
Neo Tiew Lane 136-8
Neophocaena phocaenoides 60
Nepenthes rafflesiana 133
Nephelium lappaceum 188
Nephtheidae Family 68
Neptunia plena 146, 149, 176, 179
Neptune's Cup 61, 76
Nerita spp. 64
polita 69
Neurothemis fluctuans 129
Ng Siew Yin 30
Nightjar, Large-tailed 167
Niven, Lawrence 30
Numenius phaeopus 99, 192
Nyireh 94
Nymphalidae Family 138
Nypa fruticans 147, 148

Oceanodroma monorhis 60
Octocorallia 4
Oecophylla smaragdina 176, 178
Oilfruit, Rusty 124
Olive, Spiny Black 165
Orchard Road 160, 166, 195, 197, 201
Orchid, Pigeon 40, 41, 130
Oreochromis mossambicus 139
Oriole, Black-naped 136, 158
Oriolus chinensis 136, 158
Orthotomus sepium 183

Osprey 50, 140
Otter, Smooth-coated 51, 95, 101, 105
Otus bakkamoena 167
Ovulidae Family 68
Ovum cowrie 68
Owl, Barn 167
Oyster, Leaf 97

Pachyseris rugosa 82
Palm, Australian Foxtail 156
Nipah 147, 148
Sealingwax 148
Pandanus spp. 148, 198
Pandion haliaetus 50
Pangolin, Malayan 168, 169
Pansy, Blue 166, 192
Papillidiopsis bruchii 151
Paradoxurus hermaphroditus 18, 169
Parakeet, Long-tailed 136, 195
Paraserianthes falcataria 183
Parasol, Common 129
Parathelphusa reticulata 139
Park Connectors 46
Pasir Ris Park 88, 95
Passer montanus 159
Pearl's Hill 29
Pelargopsis capensis 142
Pentaceraster mammilatus 56
Perepat 100
Periophthalmodon schlosseri 106, 107
Periophthalmus walailakae 106
Perisesarma spp. 107, 108
Pernis ptilorynchus 50, 51, 162
Phereoeca uterella 165
Pica miniaceus 176
Picus vittatus 136
Pigeon, Feral 156, 159
Pink-necked Green 176
Pipit, Paddyfield 170
Pit Viper, Mangrove 97, 108, 109
pitcher plants 22.130, 133
Pitta, Mangrove 87, 95, 104
Pitta megarhyncha 87, 95, 104
Plant, Sensitive 179
Plexippus paykulli 165
Ploceus philippinus 176
Pomacea canaliculata 152
porcelain crabs 69
Porcellanidae Family 69
Porcupine, Malayan 128
Porphyrio indicus 136
Porpoise, Finless 60
Portia Tree 24
Portunidae Family 85

Pouteria obovata 112
Poyan 130-3
Prawn, Torrent 151
Presbytis cristata 18
femoralis 123, 146, 149
melalophos 149
Prinsep, Charles 26
Prionailurus bengalensis 128
Protoreaster nodosus 54, 56
Psittacula longicauda 136
Psychodidae Family 165
Pteraeolidia ianthina 78, 79
Pteropus vampyrus 33
Ptychozoon kuhli 125
Puffinus pacificus 60
Pulau Bukom 35, 54, 56, 63, 77, 101
Pulau Hantu 77, 80
Pulau Pawai 109
Pulau Sakeng 101
Pulau Satumu 57, 59, 81
Pulau Sekudu 45
Pulau Semakau 53, 54, 56, 63, 72, 75, 87, 96, 101, 103
Pulau Tekong 104, 109, 125, 151
Pulau Tekukor 23, 37, 43
Pulau Ubin 23, 43, 44, 45, 59, 66, 72, 75, 103, 104, 105
Purseglove, John 30
Putat Sungei 24
Pycnonotus goiavier 159, 172
zeylanicus 196
Python, Reticulated 50, 195, 196

Quantula striata 129

Raffles, Thomas Stamford 17, 18, 22, 25, 111, 120
Raffles Lighthouse 57, 59, 81
Raffles Museum 33, 51, 149
Rafflesia 18
Rail, Slaty-breasted 170
Rain Tree 15, 21
Rallina fasciata 195
Rambutan 188
Rana catesbiana 139
Ratufa affinis 18
Ray, Blue-spotted Fantail 79
Spotted Eagle 79
Redshank 90, 99
Reef Crab, Red-eyed 63
reefs 41, 63, 76-80
Rhacophorus cyanopunctatus 151
Rhododendron, Straits 4, 166
Rhizophora spp. 93

stylosa 95
Rhodamnia cinerea 130
Ridley, Henry 17, 30, 31, 33, 176, 184
Robinson, Herbert 17, 33
Rostanga bifurcata 78, 79
rubber 33, 175, 184

St John's Island 35, 66
Sally Lightfoot crab 67
Salmacis sphaeroides 54
Sambar Deer 41, 51, 128, 197
Sandpiper, Marsh 90
  Spoonbill 195
Sandstone formations 43
Sand Dollar, Cake 73
  Laganum 73
Saraca declinata 194
Scaphium macropodum 123
Scartelaos histophorus 107
Scatophaga argus 139
Scops-owl, Collared 167
Scotophilus kuhlii 167
Screwpine 148
Seaslug, Strawberry 78, 79
Sea-eagle, White-bellied 50, 136, 140, 192
sea anemone, bumpy-bodied 99
sea fans 4, 66
Sea Krait, Yellow-lipped 84
Sea Pelawan 130
sea slaters 68
Sea Star, Common 75
  Knobbly 54, 56
  Mamillate 56
Sea Urchin, White 54
seagrass meadows 54, 63, 70, 72
Seagrass, Noodle 56
  Tape 53
Seletar 22, 23, 43, 140, 187
Semakau Landfill 87, 101, 103
Sentosa 37, 57, 66, 75
Sesarmine Crab, Face-banded 107, 108
Shama, White-rumped 112
Shearwater, Wedge-tailed 60
Shield Bug, Mangrove 90
Shoveler, Northern 195
Silverside, Tropical 85
Simpoh Air 49, 136, 170, 171
Singapore
  animals, statistics 50-1
  Blue Plan 197
  climatic conditions 39-40
  fish resources 59
  geology 43

Grand Prix circuit 188
green buildings 160
Green Plan 197
Index of Cities' Biodiversity 191, 198
intertidal zone 62-3
land reclamation 36, 45
landcover type map 36
map of 6
mukim districts 187
Nature Reserves 47
physical geography 36
plants, statistics 48-9
population statistics 46
rainfall 39, 40
reservoirs 140
settlement of 18-19, 22
shipping 57
size comparisons 37
tidal range 41, 43
Singapore Botanic Gardens 12, 30, 31, 33, 48, 176
Singapore Straits 59, 60, 63
Sisters Islands 35, 41, 43
Skink, Common Sun 127
Skua, Pomarine 60
Slater, Sea 66
Slider, Red-eared 135
Sloanea javanica 148
Snail, Button 76
  Golden Apple 152
  Green Tree 151
Snipe, Common 170
  Pintail 170
Sonneratia alba 100, 109
Sousa chinensis 60
Spathodea campanulata 186
Spider, Fighting 165
Spizaetus cirrhatus 50, 136
sponges 68
Squirrel, Cream-coloured Giant 18
  Plantain 187
Starling, Asian Glossy 159, 186
Stercorarius spp. 60
  pomarinus 60
Sterna albifrons 54, 59, 163
  aleutica 59
  anaethetus 59, 60
  bengalensis 133
  sumatrana 59
Stichodactyla gigantea 85
Storm-petrel, Swinhoe's 60
Streptopelia chinensis 136
  tranquebarica 136
Strix seloputo 167
Sunbird, Olive-backed 158, 159

Suncus murinus 158
Sungei Buloh Wetland Reserve 47, 88-90, 105, 192
Sungei Jelutong 45
Sungei Poyan 130
Sus scrofa 4, 41, 50, 51
Swallow, Barn 133, 171, 172
  Pacific 183
Swamphen, Black-backed 136
Swan Lake 12
Swietenia macrophylla 15
Syngnathidae Family 88
Syringodium isoetifolium 56

Tabebuia pallida 156
  rosea 156
Tachypleus gigas 99
Taeniura lymma 79
Tailorbird, Ashy 183
Tampines Eco Green 176-8
Tampoi 116
Tan Wee Kiat 30
Tembusu 33
Terminalia catappa 183
Tern, Aleutian 59
  Black-naped 59
  Bridled 59, 60
  Lesser Crested 133
  Little 54, 59, 163
  White-winged 138
Terumbu Bemban 103
Terumbu Semakau 72
Tetrathema irregularis 151
Thespesia populnea 24
Thais bitubercularis 64
Thalassina spp. 97
Thiania bhamoensis 165
Thyropygus spp. 127
Tilapia, Mozambique 139
Toa Payoh Town Park 152, 153
Todirhamphus chloris 133
Toxotes spp. 88
  jaculatix 88
Tragulus kanchil 41, 128
Trapezia cymodoce 82
Tree-oyster, Asiatic 64
Tree-shrew, Common 18
Tree Snail, Green 151
Tree-sparrow, Eurasian 159
Treetop Walk 47
Treron vernans 176
Trichoglossus haematodus 158
Trigona spp. 194
Triller, Pied 136
Tringa nebularia 90, 99
  stagnatalis 90
  totanus 90, 99

Tristania obovata 130
Tulip Tree, African 186
Tumu 94
Tupaia glis ferruginea 18
Turnera subulata 166
  ulmifolia 166
Turnera, Yellow 166
Tursiops aduncus 60
Turtle, Green 76
  Hawksbill 76
Typha angustifolia 156, 165, 166
Tyto alba 167

Uca spp. 107, 108
Umbonium vestiarium 76
Utricularia spp. 170

Vanellus indicus 170
Varanus salvator 88, 108
Vespa tropica 130
Victoria regina 27, 29
Vine, Coral 194
Vitex pinnata 114
Viverra zibetha 128
Volute, Noble 72
Vulture, Himalayan Griffon 195

Wallace, Alfred Russel 12, 14-15, 16, 127
Wang Dayuan 19
Wasp, Tropical Malayan 130
Waterhen, White-breasted 156, 170
Watersnake, Dog-faced 97, 108, 109
Wattle, Black or Hickory 176
Weaver, Baya 176
Whale, Bryde's 60
  Pygmy Sperm 60
Whampoa, H.A.K. 27, 29
Whimbrel 99, 192
Wood-owl, Spotted 167
Woodpecker, Banded 176
  Laced 136
  Sunda Pygmy 156

Xylocarpus spp. 93
Xylocopa latipes 114
Xylocopus spp. 49, 180
  rumphii 94

Yellow, Three-spot Grass 136

Zizina otis 193
zooxanthellae 81, 82, 83
Zoysia matrella 170

This edition published in the United Kingdom in 2019 by
John Beaufoy Publishing,

11 Blenheim Court, 316 Woodstock Road,

Oxford OX2 7NS, England

www.johnbeaufoy.com

10 9 8 7 6 5 4 3 2 1

ISBN 978-1-912081-10-3

Original design by Stonecastle Graphics
Cover design by Nigel Partridge
Cartography by William Smuts
Project management by Rosemary Wilkinson

Printed and bound in Malaysia by Times Offset (M) Sdn. Bhd.